You Might Be A
Geezer

Larry Vandeventer

Bloomington, IN  Milton Keynes, UK

authorHOUSE™

AuthorHouse™
1663 Liberty Drive, Suite 200
Bloomington, IN 47403
www.authorhouse.com
Phone: 1-800-839-8640

AuthorHouse™ UK Ltd.
500 Avebury Boulevard
Central Milton Keynes, MK9 2BE
www.authorhouse.co.uk
Phone: 08001974150

First published by AuthorHouse 11/30/2011

ISBN: 978-1-4259-1275-8 (sc)

Printed in the United States of America
Bloomington, Indiana

This book is printed on acid-free paper.

Table of Contents

Other Books By The Author

"There's A Booger In There and other Little Audrey Stories"

*****

"Life in The Past Lane"

*****

"Bumps In The Road (Things I Have Run Across)"

Endorsement

Wendell Trogdon, author and retired managing editor and columnist of the Indianapolis News, said nice things about my ideas on Geezers.

"Larry Vandeventer introduces us to a cast of delightful bucolic characters – 'Geezers', he calls them -- who make us forget the perils of the moment. Relax in an old rocking chair and return to a time when life was less complex, friendship more genuine and humor was tasteful, not trenchant."

****

Illustrations
by my good friend and
Christian brother

DannyGill

Introduction

This is a book about Geezers written from the perspective of a Geezer. There is an article in the AARP [American Association of Retired People] Constitution that states ***"Thou shalt not writeth about Geezers or maketh sporteth of them unless thou art one thyself."*** (King James Version) Lest you think I am twitterpated, not only am I a Geezer, I am a Hillbilly Geezer who has lived more than 13 lustrums or lustra. A lustrum, for those who are still learning, is five years. Do the math yourself.

Most of the subject matter in this book has been grown in the fertile fields of my mind and reside in my ten gazillion-gigabyte memory.

Some of the subject matter has been gleaned from a variety of sources. Ideas have flowed in on the crest of the Internet River -- the greatest incubator of plagiarism known to humanity. Some have flown in through the transom via paper airplane. If I knew the source or the author of the ideas used that did not originate with me, I would give that person due credit for his or her work. Since I don't, just assume that all these ideas are mine.

Disclaimer: *Acting on the advice of my legal counsel, Geezer, Breezer, Feezer, Freezer, Squeezer, Tweezer, Wheezer and Gelatinous, Esq., I hereby release myself from any liabilities associated with plagiarism direct or implied. Any legal concerns or matters concerning equanimity, verisimilitude, prevarication, equivocation, torts, retorts or jelly filled torts are directed to their office.*

Erudite readers will note that the print is larger than usual for the benefit of those who don't need glasses but for some reason the light is not very good in here.

So pull up an easy chair, get a glass of iced tea with lemon and sit a spell with me as I take a humorous look at those of us who are older than the posted speed limit.

Be of good cheer. Laugh and the world laughs with you, cry and you soon run out of tissues especially if colds or the flu have been going around in your family lately.

> Be Well
> Laugh Often
> Love Much

The Geezer's of OLd
Mount Rush-No-More

Part One

This Section Is About Geezers

What Is A Geezer?

I used to laugh at geezers now I am one so I have to laugh with them. Just what is a geezer? Geezers are hard to categorize and define since they are so dissimilar. They come in all shapes and sizes and surprisingly they can be all ages.

Geezer usually refers to an old man but in this book it may not be gender specific. A geezer is an older person who dresses funny. A geezer acts zany. A geezer laughs at things that other people don't think are funny at all. Geezers think heavy metal is a large tractor or bulldozer. Geezers don't have mortgage payments but their medicine bills are as much or more than their mortgage payment used to be.

Geezers use phrases like "that used to be and now its" and "before it was, it was". Elzy said,

"That used to be a Ford garage and now it's an auction barn." Audley said, "Before it was an antique store, it was a hardware store." Geezers like to meet at the barbershop and gasconade [exaggerate the truth] and gripe about the government. Geezers are out of the mainstream of life and that is perfectly all right with them. They remember the stress of the work-a-day world and are glad to be out of it. When I think of Geezers I think of a bunch of older men like Burt, Al, Floyd and Charlie, who used to hang around the streets of Mayberry and drive Barney Fife crazy.

So now you have an idea of what a Geezer is. Read on and learn to love Geezers. You may be one yourself some day. You will be if you live long enough. Just ask the tsunami of Baby Boomers who are just beginning to crash onto the beach at AARPville.

How to Recognize a Geezer!

It is crucial that you are able to recognize a geezer. The thought has occurred to me that sometimes you might not know if you are talking to a Geezer because they can disguise themselves. It is important to know since geezers and normal people share the same language but don't necessarily share the same vocabulary. One must learn to compensate for the dearth of knowledge that non-geezers have. How do you know you are talking with a Geezer?

Geezers say, "I won't ride with Esther any more because she can't see or hear. Everybody in town cringes when they see Arthur coming. He is going to kill someone some day and get himself killed in the process."

Conversation among a group of geezers is like instant replay in the NFL. Don't be alarmed if you didn't hear it the first time, invariably someone will say, "What" or "Huh", and the statement will be replayed, sometimes more than once. But no one needs a hearing aid, right?

Geezers amuse themselves differently. Most senior centers have connect-the-dot day where people use magic markers to connect the liver spots on the back of their hands. One old guy I know claims that he can outline Uncle Sam on his hand. Okay, I did it. Once.

Last night you watched Survivor or the Sopranos or Victoria's Secret, Sex in the City or Ringing in the New Year at the Playboy Mansion. You ask, "Did you see the show last night?" The person replies, "Yes I did. That Goober is so funny. Or, isn't Nellie a hateful little girl?" An alarm should sound in your head that the person you are talking to is a Geezer. The Geezer then said that he also watched Mary Tyler Moore, Lawrence Welk, Leave it to Beaver, I Love Lucy and the Waltons. If you didn't know that Goober is in the Andy Griffith Show and Nellie is in Little House On The Prairie, you may not be a Geezer.

Geezers have a mantra about television shows. They loudly proclaim with great conviction that none of those other shows are fit to watch. They add that there is too much sex, violence, vulgarity and profanity in those filthy shows. Many geezers feel that the "Waltons" have almost crossed the line now with Jimmy Bob playing his guitar in a roadhouse and the two sisters making the recipe. Everyone just looks the other way because they are nice little old ladies but they are moonshiners! It is sad that many geezers don't realize that the Waltons Show is in syndication now and that John Boy is 79 years old and living on social security in Brooklyn in a room that you pay by the week.

Geezers are out of the fashion loop. Calvin Klein, Boss, Old Navy and Abercrombie and Fitch are just people they went to school with or who were in the service with them. If the person you are speaking to is wearing a leisure suit or double knit bell bottomed pants and platform shoes, you are walking the streets of "Geezerville."

Geezers take large amounts of medicine. They all have those specially manufactured containers with days of the week embossed on the flip top lids. If the lid is up and the box is empty they know they have taken their medicine. And, if they go anywhere, they carry their medicine in those hard-side blue or green Samsonite overnight cases with a mirror in the lid. Geezers go into great detail about the many times they have been "under the knife." Someone will invariably state that Anna Clifford has hyperactoliphomea! Katie bar the door. Now there is a term that identifies the speaker as a geezer.

Geezers transfuse every conversation with out of left field statements such as, "Did you hear that Charlie dropped dead out in the barn?" Or, "Did you know that the drugstore is going to close?" And, "The doctor opened Ned up and just sewed him back together." Plus, "Did you hear that Lois is going in for hemorrhoid surgery tomorrow in Bloomington?" Thank you for that bulletin.

You know you are in Geezerville when there is something wrong with every restaurant in the area. They say such things as we went to Bob's "Gravy over Everything" Café once and the food was so cold we couldn't eat it and the waitress added the tip onto the bill for our group of 18 and some people didn't like it. Or, the service is too slow, the food isn't cooked properly, they serve booze, they are closed on Monday or Tuesday, portions are too large or too small, overpriced, too smoky, the silverware isn't clean and their instant tea tastes like swamp water.

Now you should be able to identify a Geezer? Let's all sing together now, "I'm a Geezer, she's a geezer, he's a geezer, someday you will be a geezer too?" This has been a public service announcement.

Geezer Guffaws

I have included some Geezer jokes, groaners, shaggy dog stories, anecdotes and guffaws for your reading pleasure.

- Regulations at Community Hospital require a wheelchair for patients being discharged. One day, Anne, working as a student nurse, found one elderly gentleman – already dressed and sitting on the bed with a suitcase at his feet – who insisted he didn't need her help to leave the hospital. She had a chat with him about rules being rules, so Amsey let her wheel him to the elevator. On the way down she asked him if his wife was meeting him.

Amsey replied, "I don't know, I think she's still upstairs in the bathroom changing out of her hospital gown."

- Geezer Elmo was driving down the freeway, and his cell phone rang. The first funny part about this is that Elmo would have a cell phone. He answered and heard his wife's voice urgently warning him, "Elmo, I just heard on the news that there is a car going the wrong way on I-74. Please be careful!"

"Expletive deleted," said Elmo, "It's not just one car. It's hundreds of them!"

- Three retirees were playing golf one fine April day. They all had degrees of hearing loss. Elzy said, "Windy, isn't it?" Amsey replied, "It's Thursday." Audley chimed in, "So am I. Let's stop at the nineteenth hole and have a Bubble Up."

- Beverly and Janet had been members of the Red Hat Society and friends for many decades. They had shared many activities and adventures. Lately their activities had been limited to meeting a few times a week to play cards. One day they were playing cards when Beverly looked at Janet and said, "Now don't get mad at me, I know we have been friends for a long time but I just can't think of your name! I've thought and thought, but I can't remember it. Please tell me what your name is." Janet glared at her. For at least three minutes she just stared and glared at her. Finally she said, "How soon do you need to know?"

- Mildred and Ruth were out driving in a big ole' Buick. Cars come in three sizes: small, large and big ole'. They could barely see over the dashboard. As they were cruising along, they came to an intersection. The stoplight was red, but they just went on through.

  Ruth, in the passenger seat thought, "I must be losing my mind. I could have sworn we just went through a red light." After a few more minutes they came to another intersection and the light was red again. Again they went right through. Ruth was almost sure that the light had been red but was really concerned that she was losing her mind. She was getting nervous and decided to pay very close attention to the road and the next intersection.

  At the next intersection, sure enough, the light was red and they went on through. So she turned and said,

"Mildred, did you know that we just ran through three red lights in a row? You could have killed us both!"

Mildred turned to her and said, "Oh my, am I driving?"

- One evening a family brought their frail, elderly father to the nursing home to leave him, hoping he would receive proper care.

  The next morning, attendants bathed him, fed him a tasty breakfast and set him in a chair at a window overlooking a lovely flower garden. He seemed okay, but after a while he slowly started to lean over sideways in his chair. Two attentive attendants immediately rushed up to catch him and straighten him up. He seemed all right for a time.

  After a while he started to tilt to the other side. The attendants rushed back and once more brought him back upright. That went on all morning. Later the family arrived to see how the old fellow was adjusting to his new home.

  "Hello, Dad, how is it here? Are they treating you all right?" Susan asked.

  "It's pretty nice," he said, "Except they won't let you fart."

- Eighty-year-old Bertha burst into the recreation room at the retirement home. She held her clenched fist in the air and announced, "Anyone who can guess what's in my hand can have a date with me tonight with a guaranteed good night kiss!"

  Audley in the rear shouted, "An elephant!"

  Bertha thought a moment and said, "Close enough."

- Three Sisters, Maude 92, Chloe 94 and Sarah 96 live in a house together. One night Sarah drew a bath. She put one foot in and paused and yelled down the stairs, "Was I getting in or out of the bath?"

  Maude yelled back, "I don't know. I'll come up there and see." She started up the stairs and paused, then, she yelled, "Was I going up the stairs or down the stairs?"

  Chloe, who was sitting at the kitchen table having tea, listening to her sisters, shook her head and said, "I sure hope I never get that forgetful," and knocked on wood for good measure. She then yelled, "I'll come up and help both of you as soon as I see who is at the door."

- Roy said, "I had an anaconda snake that I named Julius Squeezer. When he got old I renamed him Julius Geezer."

- Bert and Grace, an older couple, were lying in bed one night. Bert was falling asleep but Grace was in a romantic mood and wanted to talk. She said, "You used to hold my hand when we were courting."

  Wearily Bert reached across, held her hand for a second and tried to get back to sleep.

  A few moments later Grace said, "Then you used to kiss me." Mildly irritated, Bert reached across, gave her a peck on the cheek and settled down again to sleep.

  Thirty seconds later Grace said, "Then you used to bite my neck."

  Angrily, he threw back the bed covers and got out of bed.

  "Where are you going?" Grace asked.

  "To get my teeth."

- One night as she was preparing for bed, Grandma Perkins was slathering her face with cream and unguents. Jessica, her granddaughter was watching and she asked, "Why do you put that stuff on your face?" Grandma replied, "It helps to remove wrinkles." Jessica looked and pondered for a moment and said, "I don't mean to hurt your feelings but it isn't working."

- Two AARPers from a retirement center were sitting on a bench under a tree when Elzy turned to Elmo and said, "Elmo, I'm 85 years old now and I'm just full of aches and pains. I know you're about my age. How do you feel?" Elmo replied, "I feel just like a new-born baby." Elzy exclaimed, "Really? Like a new-born baby!" "Yep. No hair, no teeth and I think I just wet my pants."

- One day Joey asked his grandfather to help him with his math. Grandpa said, "Sure I'll help. What do you need?" Joey said, "I am supposed to find the lowest common denominator for this problem." Grandpa said, "Are they still looking for the lowest common denominator? They were looking for that when I was in school."

- Grandma put her two grandchildren to bed and changed into an old sweat suit and proceeded to wash her hair. As she heard the children getting more and more rambunctious, her patience grew thin. At last she threw a towel around her head and stormed into their room, put them back into bed with a stern warning to go to sleep. As she left the room, she heard the three-year old say with a trembling voice, "Who was that?" Grandma had to sit down and laugh awhile.

- Grandma didn't know if her granddaughter had learned her colors yet, so she decided to test her. She would point out something and ask what color is that. Annie would look and tell her the correct color each time. It was fun for granny so she continued. At last Annie started to leave and as she went to the door she said sagaciously, "Grandma, I think you should try to figure out some of these colors yourself."

- Five-year old Mark couldn't wait to tell his grandfather about the movie he had just watched on television, "20,000 Leagues Under the Sea." The scenes with the submarine and the giant octopus had kept him wide-eyed. In the middle of the telling, his grandfather interrupted Mark and asked, "What caused the submarine to sink?" With a look of incredulity Mark replied, "It was the 20,000 leaks!"

- Grandpa and grandson Billy sneaked into the lake cottage in the dark to keep the mosquitoes and other insects from coming in with them. A few fireflies followed them in anyway. Billy noticed them before his Grandpa and whispered, "It's no use grandpa. The mosquitoes are coming after us with flashlights."

- A grandson asked his grandmother, "How old are you?" Grandma teasingly replied, "I'm not sure." He said, "Look inside your underwear, Grandma, mine says I'm four."

- While on a road trip, Audley and Esther stopped at a roadside restaurant for lunch. After finishing their meal, they left the restaurant and resumed their trip. When leaving, Esther unknowingly left her glasses on the table, and she didn't miss them until after they had been driving about twenty minutes. By then, to add to the aggravation, they had to travel quite a distance before they could find a place to turn around in order to return to the restaurant to retrieve her glasses.

All the way back, Audley became the classic grouchy old man. He fussed and complained and scolded his wife relentlessly

The more he chided her the more agitated she became. He just wouldn't let up for one minute. Esther was greatly relieved when they finally arrived at the restaurant. As she got out of the car and hurried inside to retrieve her glasses, Audley yelled to her, "While you're in there, you might as well get my hat, and credit card."

Birthdays Are Good For You - -Especially Geezers

Old is a relative term. I should know. Many of my relatives are old. So is Geezer Town. If you are a 17-year cicada you are under ground for 17 years, come out and turn into a green eyed, winged ugly creature, sing for three or four weeks then die. Imagine cicadas talking at the barbershop. Did you see Earl yesterday? He didn't look very good. He must be three weeks old now.

I've been doing some reflecting and ruminating about being old. I still believe that old age is ten years older than you are no matter how old you are. One of my old buddies is Frank. He is so old he remembers Preparation "B." His white corpuscles are tattletale gray. One day he was almost hit by a train at the downtown crossing and he said, after his heart returned to a normal rate, that his whole life flashed before his eyes. He was surprised to find that his life was a blooper reel that Dick Clark wanted to use for his TV show.

You know where Geezer Blvd. is and you just may live there if the following describes you and your friends.

- ❑ You enjoy the company of the telemarketer and talk with him for 30 minutes.
- ❑ People call at 9 p.m. and ask, "Did I wake you?" and you have to admit they did.
- ❑ You call young people at 5:00 in the morning and ask, "Did I wake you?" and you did.
- ❑ The likelihood of being kidnapped is very remote.
- ❑ If you should be taken hostage, you will be released quickly as being of no worth.
- ❑ You are no longer perceived as a hypochondriac.
- ❑ At some time or other you think you have every new malady discussed on "60 Minutes."

- You enjoy hearing about other peoples' operations and infirmities and think, I am sure glad I don't have that.
- You get into heated arguments about pension plans.
- You no longer think of speed limits as a challenge
- You quit trying to hold your stomach in, no matter who walks into the room.
- Nobody gives you the once over when you come into the room.
- You wear shoes for comfort not style.
- Your eye sight won't get much worse.
- You have "saucered" and "blowed" coffee or watched someone do it.
- You carry your own toothpick.
- You have eaten boiled blackberry cobbler.
- You wanted/have a shiny gold front tooth and you aren't a rapper.
- You go out to paint the town red but you can only find green; you have to be home by dark any way.
- You like to eat cornbread and milk and crackers and milk.
- You think an old timer is a Grandfather Clock.
- All that money you invested in health insurance is finally beginning to pay off.

❑ Your long-term health care insurance gives you some long-term financial comfort.

❑ You begin the process of selecting a drug discount card from any pharmacy.

❑ Your joints are more accurate meteorologists than the national weather bureau

❑ Your secrets are safe with your friends, because they can't remember them either.

❑ Your working number of brain cells is finally down to manageable size

❑ You have 120 stations on your cable service but there is nothing on fit to watch.

❑ You watch the new and exciting career promotions on TV from ITT Tech and Brown College and Midwest Bartending School and decide that you are not interested.

❑ You read the Oscar nominees and winners in the paper and realize that you don't recognize any of the names and you haven't seen any of the movies.

❑ Although you have a university degree you can't remember the last time a headhunter made contact with you.

❑ You spend almost as much on medicine and doctor bills each month as you once spent on your mortgage payments.

❑ You reach the conclusion that your grandchildren are smarter, cuter, more advanced, more talented than anyone else's and maybe even your own children at that age.

❏ Florida in December, January, February and March sounds better all the time.

❏ Maybe the reason you can't sleep through the night could be that long daily nap you take.

❏ You have all the answers to life's problems but no one asks for your advice.

❏ You'd rather baby sit with your grand-daughter than go to any movie.

❏ When asked, "Coffee, tea or me?" you select the coffee or tea.

❏ An evening of cozy, warm, snuggling is compliments of a heavy quilt or electric blanket.

❏ Your cholesterol count is more important to you than where the Cardinals stand in the National League.

❏ You can point to the precise place on your arm where blood samples are taken. In fact, there is a perennial red dot left by previous needles.

❏ Your eyeglasses are way out of style but you don't care as long as you can see.

❏ You know the difference between a cataract and a Cadillac.

- To you putting the pedal to the metal means you dropped a flower in the kitchen sink.

- Those assisted hearing devices offered at the theater seem like a good idea.

- Your Johnny Walker has nothing to do with distilled spirits and everything to do with getting to the necessary at night.

- When your house gets the same temperature in the summer, as you like to keep it in winter you turn on the air conditioning and then wear the same sweater you wear in the winter.

- There are so many nightlights on in your house at night that pilots confuse your place with the landing strip at Indy International.

- You make more trips down the hall to Ft. Necessity at night than the noon food cart at Methodist Hospital.

Geezer Problems In 2005

Geezers have sure taken their lumps this past year. They have difficulty maneuvering through the minefields of life without being blown to bits. I have been the clearinghouse for maintaining data on the travails of my fellow Geezers. Later this year I will be called before a Senate Sub-committee and representatives from AARP to share my data.

- ❑ Gertrude Geezer returned a Christmas scarf to the store because it was too tight.
- ❑ Grampa Geezer tried to learn to water ski but he couldn't find a lake with a slope so he failed.
- ❑ Helen had to leave her job in a pharmacy because the bottles wouldn't fit into the typewriter so she could type the instructions on the label.

- Arlo and Arnell became so excited because they finished a jigsaw puzzle in six months and the box said two to four years.

- Lulu was trapped on an escalator in Sears for hours when the power went off.

- Thurlow couldn't call 911 because there was no eleven on any phone button.

- When asked what is the capital of Indiana Gaylord answered "I."

- Poor old Maude Hillstrop burned her nose bobbing for French fries.

- Maizie Mayberry is not the brightest bulb in the chandelier. She baked a turkey for six days because the instructions said bake one hour per pound and she weighs 150.

- Claude Resin decided he couldn't make Kool-Aid for his grandchildren because the little packets of flavor cannot hold eight cups of water.

- Clovis Clevis loves chocolate but he hates M&Ms because they are so hard to peel.

- Al Glass hurt himself while raking leaves. He fell out of the tree.

- Granny Whistle doesn't understand the new disposable diapers. She only changed the grandbaby's diaper every day or so because the label said "Good for up to 20 pounds."

❑ Ethel and Louise take aquatic exercise classes at the YMCA. They entered the breaststroke swimming competition and lost. Ethel complained that the other swimmers were using their arms.

❑ What goes "vroom-screech-vroom-screech-vroom-screech? Clue and Less Geezer at a flashing red light

❑ Fred and Dwight Geezer were trying to get into their car using a coat hanger to unlock the door when Fred said to Dwight, "We better hurry, Dwight, it's starting to rain and the top is down."

❑ Dorman Rivers went to the doctor because his right knee was hurting. The doctor took and x-ray, MRI, TGIF, PBLA, NFL and WPA and found nothing to explain the pain. He said, "Dorman, it must be your age." Dorman said, "It cain't be Doc, my left knee is the same age and it don't hurt a bit."

❑ Elmo had a heat stroke in July and almost died. He was painting his barn wearing two winter coats, gloves and a woolen cap. The EMT group revived him on the way to the hospital and asked him why he was dressed that way. Elmo replied, "Well, the instructions on the can said to put on two coats!"

- Amsey and Ethel were going to the Smoky Mountains for a vacation. They crossed the line into Tennessee when suddenly Amsey threw a sack of trash out of the window. Unluckily a state trooper witnessed the event and gave him a ticket for littering. Amsey protested, "I just saw a sign that said 'fine for littering', so this place looked about as good as any I've seen, so I chunked that stuff out the window."

- Elzy was elected to the town board and with his leadership they finally painted a yellow line down the middle of Main Street. However, every time it rained, it washed off the gravel.

- Audley is so old that last Halloween he didn't have his teeth with him so he bobbed for applesauce.

- Elwood was talking to Elrod, "My wife gripes all of the time." Elrod asked, "What's she gripin' about?" "She was wanting a washer and a dryer. So, I finally gave in and bought her a set. But she's still griping. Now she's wantin' electricity and runnin' water!"

- My Uncle Lonzo has a new hairdo. He parts it from ear to ear. He combs the front part forward and the back part backward. I asked him how he liked his new hairdo. He said, "I like it pretty good but I get tired of people whispering in my nose."

Welcome Home Geezer

My wife and I have been considering purchasing property in Florida so we can spend the winter there. There are only two reasons we haven't done so already. The first reason is the cost and that is also the second reason. We already own property in Geezerville. Yes, you may own property in Geezerville if you have experienced more than one of the following situations.

- ❏ The doctor removed a large wax deposit from your left ear and you felt dehydrated
- ❏ Your friends compliment you on your new alligator shoes and you're barefoot
- ❏ You are really happy at being regular but being unstoppable is something else.

- ❑ Hollywood released a new historical movie and you can't concentrate on it because the characters don't look like the real people because you remember them.
- ❑ You watch old newsreels on the History channel and reminisce because you were there.
- ❑ The high point of your day is when the newspaper and mail are delivered.
- ❑ The high point of the week is trash pick-up day.
- ❑ The high point of the month is when your social security and retirement checks are electronically transferred to the bank.
- ❑ Your high school classmates have become so old and wrinkled they don't recognize you.
- ❑ All of your liver spots coalesce into one spot and you now look like Michael Jackson used to look.
- ❑ You can tick off the names of all of your deceased high school classmates.
- ❑ For the last four years you have recognized all of the people in the 50th class reunions because they were in school just ahead of you. You are next.

- You remember the names of all of Elizabeth Taylor's husbands but can't remember your social security number that you have had since you were sixteen.

- You remember all of the cars you have owned but can't remember to take your medicine on time.

- You clearly remember your wedding day and night but forget your anniversary. Ouch.

- You remember when birthdays were fun and you wanted them to come quickly.

- You remember what items used to cost but forget how low your income was.

- You remember when you couldn't wait for Santa Claus to come and now you are Santa Claus and you feel a little tired and less enthusiastic about the 25th of December.

- You remember thinking, "I will never look like or talk like my parents." Surprise!

- You remember when Match Game '75, The Lucy Show and The Waltons were on prime time but forget your son-in-law's birthday.

- That little bump on your back has turned into a wart that you could hang a picture on.

- Your fingernails have more ridges and grooves on them than the Smoky Mountains
- You have more hair in your ears and nose than on your head.
- Your back looks like a field of waving wheat and your head looks like a bowling ball.
- You copied your favorite recipes on new cards and now you can't find your favorite ones.
- You glance in a store window and notice an old, fat, bald guy walking near you and you realize that it is your own reflection.
- Your doctor said that you have a sebaceous keratosis on your head and you hope it will hide your bald spot.
- You go streaking down the hall and someone suggests that you should iron your outfit.
- A sexy babe catches your fancy and your pacemaker opens the garage door
- Going bra-less pulls all the wrinkles out of your face.
- You don't care where your spouse goes, just as long as you don't have to go along
- You are cautioned to slow down by the doctor instead of the police

❑ Getting a little action means there is no need to take any fiber today.

❑ Getting lucky means you found your car in the parking lot at Sprawl-Mart.

❑ Pulling an all-nighter means not getting up to go to the bathroom.

❑ You know all of the songs heard on the elevator

❑ You begin to think that you might live long enough to cash in your own life insurance policy

❑ Fred tells you his cholesterol count and you think, "My word that is higher than Dow Jones."

❑ You throw a wild New Year's Eve party and the neighbors don't even realize it because everyone goes home before dark.

❑ Branson wins over Las Vegas.

❑ Singing the line of a hymn at church, "prostrate in the garden," reminds you of your next check up.

❑ If the sound of a person putting on rubber gloves makes you break out in a cold sweat

❑ You grow tired of hearing your doctor say two things: "You are getting to the age where...." and "For a man your age you are...."

"If you have more hair in your nose, ears and eyebrows than on your head, You may be a geezer."

Geezer Dictionary

Geezers just plain talk funny. Especially Geezers from the country. I grew up in Poke and Plum, Indiana. Poke your head out the window and you are plum out in the sticks. It wasn't the end of the world but you could see it from there. We lived so far out we had to go toward town to hunt. Geezers use words and sounds that make sense when you hear them but in reality they don't make sense at all. Therefore, in an effort to improve communication between the generations, I have compiled an abridged Geezer Dictionary so you will understand Geezers when you talk to 'em. Remember I am just the reporter so go slow on boiling the tar and plucking the goose.

Abundance – I ain't never seen a.bun.dance but I have seen a horse fly.

Aisle - Aisle be back after work.

Andropov – I'm going around the block andropov the kids at their school.

Artificial insemination – When the farmer does it to the bull instead of the cow.

Awesome – Who was raising that ruckus last night? Awesome of those ole' boys down at the Greasy Elbow Tavern were lettin' off some steam

Bagel – That bagel hold all the stuff you need.

Banner – Elsie got so mad she threw her chitlins' at Elmo. Red Neckerson is gonna banner from the Redneck Olympic Games.

Barn – I weren't barn yesterday.

Bernadette – when you torch a mortgage.

Belittle – There'll belittle space between those 18-

wheelers on that bridge.

Benign – Benign is what you will be after you be eight

Better – The temperature got so cold last night you can better car won't start this morning.

Bifurcate – What did you bifurcate this Christmas?

Big 'ol – Small, medium, large and Big 'ol

Boiler – Is that a boiler a pimple?

Brownies – Brownies going deer huntin' down in

Tennessee tomorrow.

Buccaneer – If prices keep going up it won't be long till corn will cost a buccaneer.

Butter – She wanted to go out on a school night butter Dad wouldn't have it.

Caesarean Section – a district in Rome

Candle – I like candle pickles bettern' canned sweet pickles any day.

Capital – That was a mighty fine meal and that apple pie will capital off.

Cattle – That cattle scratch you if you pick 'er up.

Center – I was lookin' for Lori but her mom center to the store.

Circumference – Ain't he the knight that invented the round table?

Collar – I don't know where Lulu is. Why don't you collar on the phone?

Control – That ole' boy control for fish bettern'

anybody I know.

Couple – That couple break if you drop it on the floor.

Debate – this is what happens when you release the worm

Disguise – If you want to see an airplane you have to look in disguise.

Dispatch – Dispatch here is where I plant taters.

Doctor – Flo didn't go to work one day so the boss

doctor a day's pay.

Dresser – If you are taking that baby girl with us you got to dresser first.

Far – That far sure is hot.

Fascinate – There are nine buttons on this shirt but I can only fascinate.

Fibula – a small lie

Gallon – That big 'ol gallon the corner works at the post office.

Graceful – Is Graceful or does she want some more dressing.

Grudge – That there grudge ain't big enough for yer truck.

Gutter – Her poor attendance at school gutter in trouble with the principal.

Hermit – a girl's baseball glove.

Hullabaloo – when the Titanic hit the iceberg.

Inner tubes – Doc Leghorn says she has some blockage inner tubes.

Jacket – Before we change the tar on this old truck you gotta jacket up.

Letter – She wanted to go out and play but her mom wouldn't letter.

Liquor – Large Marge is a big ole' woman but I know Heavy Helen could liquor in a fair fight.

Mouse – Where do you live from here? Mouse is just around the hill there.

Muddle – We have had so much rain that muddle get all over yer car.

Noun – Noun then I go to town.

Parade – Grandma was sick so we parade for her to get well.

Parasites – When you climb up the Eiffel Tower you can see the parasites.

Pigment – That pigment no harm when he bit you. He just got excited.

Pigment – what the maid puts on Porky's pillow when she turns down his bed.

Pilot – What do you want me to do with this cow
manure? Pilot over there.

Porous – Will you porous some iced tea?

Primate – the act of pulling your wife out of Sprawl-Mart

Proper – She's ain't feeling too purty good. Proper up so she can rest better.

Ribbon – He sure can dish it out but he cain't take a ribbon himself.

Rubber – She'll get mad if you rubber the wrong way. Turn her around.

Ruffle – If the wind picks up that barn ruffle blow right off.

Saturnine – a baseball team than only plays on the weekend.

Seafood – When I seafood, I eat it.

Shutter – Give her some more fries. That'll shutter up.

Steeple – This hill is so steeple be hard to drive the team up it.

Steroids – things that keep carpets on the stairs.

Subdued – My uncle was a subdued in the Navy. He was on a submarine.

Superficial – a really great referee.

Swatter – She was bad so I had to swatter.

Tar – That back tar is going flat. You better get some air in it

Tennessee – All those other women are dogs. You are the only Tennessee.

Tolerate – Tolerate seven of them hot peppers and it liked to killed him.

Varicose – means very close, nearby

Wagon – That dog sure is happy. He's been wagon his tail all morning.

Water – Water you doing, boy?

Weird – Weird they go?

Wiggle – Her wiggle come off if the wind blows much harder.

Wok – my car quit me and I had to wok to town.

Wrinkle – a small hockey arena.

You May Not Know This But

Geezers smile when they remember singing along with the Serendipity Singers and the Back Porch Majority and they remember when the only radio stations were AM and the only stations you could get were WIBC Indianapolis, WLS in Chicago, WLW in Cincinnati, WSM and the Opry out of Nashville, WWL in New Orleans and KMOX St. Louis. They remember The Hoosier Hotshots and Captain Stubby and the Buccaneers; Red Foley and Ernest Tubb and listened to Lula Belle and Scotty on the WLS Barn Dance

❑ Geezers remember when women made dresses out of feed sacks and they thought that Red Skelton was hilarious. Shoot, they remember when women **WORE** dresses.

- Geezers know that things usually come out all right but sometimes prunes are involved and they frequently appear on the grocery list.

- Geezers actually order turnip greens at Cracker Barrel Restaurants and like them.

- It only takes three minutes for Geezers to get a haircut but they are charged the same price as everyone else. The barber chuckles and calls it a finder's fee. They also remember where all the barbershops used to be and the barber's name.

- When geezers were kids school started after Labor Day and ended in April. They remember when the teacher would call them in from noon or recess with the hand bell. Everyone knew what it meant in elementary school when you held up one or two fingers.

- Geezers aren't expected to run anywhere except to the restroom at the mall. In fact they are so old they can't even run amuck.

- Geezers remember when you could buy almost everything you needed at the general store. If they didn't have it you didn't need it. If they didn't have it, they could order it. They remember when gasoline cost 20 cents per gallon but they didn't own a car and didn't go anywhere any way.

❏ Geezers know what RFD means. They know what FDR means too.

❏ Geezers have nothing left to learn the hard way and the things they buy now won't wear out.

❏ Geezers can eat dinner at 4 p.m. or at 3:00 or whenever they want.

❏ Geezer conversations include such words as Zoot suit, daddyo, you're the most, duck tails and turned up collars.

You Live In Geezerville

It is quite interesting that sometimes Geezers are in denial and still see themselves as middle-aged or approaching middle age. However,

- ❏ If your five-passenger car still hauls five people but one of them must ride in the trunk you live in Geezerville.

- ❏ If your face looks like a cross between a basset hound and one of those Shar-pei dogs that look like it should be ironed you live in Geezerville.

- ❏ If your fingernails look like a new concrete sidewalk that has been brushed with a broom you live in Geezerville.

- ❏ If your fingernails have as many grooves as a 78 record and almost as may dings and dents you live in Geezerville.

- If you know what a 78 record is you live in Geezerville.

- If you can speak your mind but you can't remember what you were going to say you live in Geezerville.

- If you conclude that it's just easier to buy a larger belt you live in Geezerville.

- If you are convinced that clothing manufacturers put less material in clothing today but charge more for it you live in Geezerville.

- If your dollar doesn't go as far as it used to, but you'd rather stay home anyway you live in Geezerville.

- If you go into Staples and are shocked that they don't have a ribbon for your portable Underwood typewriter that you received as a high school graduation gift you live in Geezerville.

- If the clerk at Best Buy stifles a laugh when you ask if they sell needles for your RCA Gramophone you live in Geezerville.

- If your grandson graduated from Indiana University this year you live in Geezerville.

- ❏ If you have ever taken the Sears catalogue to the privy and used it for something other than placing an order, you live in Geezerville.
- ❏ If you have one of those pillboxes for each day of the week to take your medicine but can't remember what day it is you live in Geezerville.

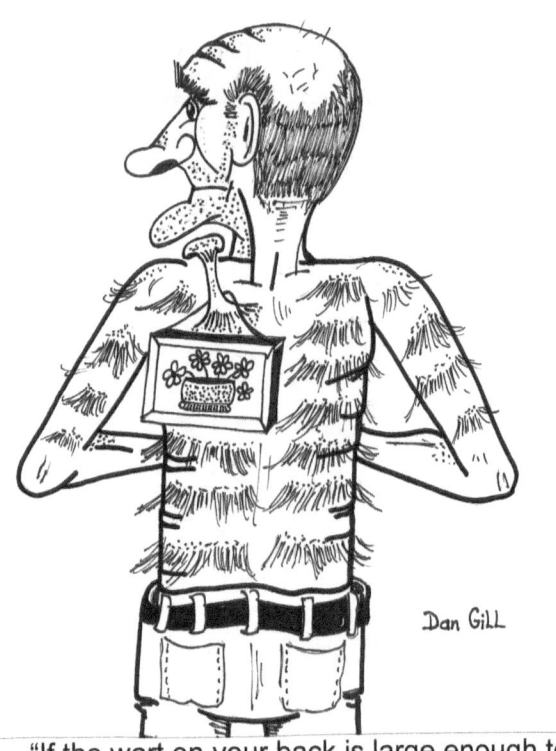

"If the wart on your back is large enough to hang a picture on it, You may be a geezer."

Dan Gill

Geezer Test!

I make no claims on the authorship of this magnificent work. It came in over the transom called the Internet. Actually my only sister-in-law, Earlene, forwarded it to me and it looks like it has been down several roads and crossed many bridges before getting to me.

Technically the statement, "You are older than dirt", is a misnomer. Even casual Bible scholars know that water existed before dirt so a more appropriate question here is "Are you older than water?" But I digress.

Do you put your glasses down and then can't find them again? Have you ever read the mail and then remember needing to respond to a letter or bill and then can't find it? Are you forever looking for your purse or car keys? Have you ever put your grand child down and forgot where you put him? You remember every persons name in your first grade classroom but you can't remember where you put the tickets for the performance tonight. You had a dental appointment yesterday but forgot and took a nap instead. If you couldn't remember your social security number when filling out your 1040 form last year and it was on the address label, maybe you are having a memory problem.

This is the quiz for you.

1. Where was the headlight dimmer switch located in older cars?
   a. On the floor shift knob
   b. On the floor, left of the clutch
   c. Next to the horn
2. Why did the bottle top of a Royal Crown Cola bottle have holes in it?
   a. To capture lightning bugs
   b. To sprinkle clothes before ironing
   c. Salt shaker
3. In northern winters home milk delivery was a problem because?
   a. Cows got cold and wouldn't produce
   b. Ice on highways forced delivery by dog sled

c.   Milkmen left deliveries outside doors and milk would freeze, expanding and pushing up the cardboard bottle top.

4. What was the name of a popular chewing gum named after a game of chance?
   a.   Blackjack
   b.   Gin
   c.   Craps

5. During W.W. II, nylon stockings were not available. What method did women adapt to look like they were wearing stockings?
   a.   Suntan
   b.   Leg painting
   c.   Wearing slacks

6. What postwar car turned the automobile design on its ear when you couldn't tell whether it was coming or going?
   a.   Studebaker
   b.   Nash metro
   c.   Tucker

7. Which was a popular candy when you were a kid?
   a.   Strips of dried peanut butter b. Chocolate-licorice bars c. Wax coke-shaped bottle with colored sugar water inside.

8. How was Butch wax used?
   a. To stiffen hair cut into a flattop
   b. To make floors shiny and prevent scuffing
   c. On the wheels of roller skates to prevent rust.

9. Before inline skates, how did you keep your roller skates attached to your shoes?
   a. With clamps, tightened by a skate key
   b. Woven straps that crossed the foot
   c. Long pieces of baling string or twine.

10. As a kid, what was considered the best way to reach a decision?
   a. Consider all facts
   b. Ask Mom
   c. Eeny-meeny-miney-mo

11. What was the worst thing you could catch from the opposite sex?
   a. A cold
   b. VD
   c. Cooties

12. "I'll be down to get you in a _____, Honey?"
   a. SUV
   b. Taxi
   c. Streetcar

13. What was the name of Caroline Kennedy's pet pony?
    a.   Old Blue
    b.   Paint
    c.   Macaroni

14. What was a Duck and Cover Drill?
    a.   Part of the game of hide and seek
    b.   What you did when your mom called you in to do chores
    c.   Hiding under your desk, covering your head with your arms in a bomb drill.

15. What was the name of the Indian Princess on the Howdy Doody Show?
    a.   Princess Summerfallwinterspring
    b.   Princess Sacajewea
    c.   Princess Moonshadow

16. What did all savvy students do when ditto tests were handed out in school?
    a.   Immediately sniffed the purple ink, as this was believed to get you "high".
    b.   Made paper airplanes to see who could sail theirs out the window.
    c.   Went straight to work to get your A

17. What were S & H Green Stamps?
    a.   Outdated stamps at the post office
    b.   Stick on tattoos
    c.   Stamps given by merchants with each purchase that could be redeemed for household items.

18. Praise the lord and pass the _____ "
   a.   Meatballs
   b.   Dames
   c.   Ammunition
19. What was the name of the group who made the song "Cab Driver" a hit?
   a.   The Ink Spots
   b.   The Supremes
   c.   The Esquires
20.   Who left his heart in San Francisco?
   a.   Tony Bennett
   b.   Xavier Cugat
   c.   George Gershwin

Scoring:

17 - 20 Correct. You are not only older than water, but obviously gifted with mind bloat. Now if you could only find your glasses.

12 - 16 Correct. Not quite dirt yet, but your mind is definitely muddy.

Answers: 1. B; 2. B; 3. C; 4. A; 5. B
6. A; 7. C; 8. A; 9. A; 10. C; 11. C; 12.
B; 13. C; 14. C; 15. A; 16. A; 17. B; 18.
C; 19. A; 20. A.

---

0 - 11 Correct. You are a sad excuse for a geezer. Redeem yourself by declaring to everyone that the world is going to hell in a hand basket and you are carrying said basket.

Part Two

Geezer
Reflections

"AARPERS" Ferry

The ferryboat is more than a vessel or boat. The term evokes memories, possibilities and opportunities. A ferryboat transports people, vehicles, and products from place to place across rivers, bays, lakes and harbors. No special roads or tracks are needed, just a boat. Harper's Ferry is renowned in American History. I want to introduce you to "AARPers" Ferry

AARPer's Ferry" is a metaphor because it is a Time Machine that is able to escape the surly bonds of the present. It carries its passengers along the River of Time from Yesterday Bay through Reminisce Harbor and docks at Pier Today and has the capacity to make the return trip. Strange vessel, it also makes stops along the way and even takes some flights of fancy

to tomorrow. The excursions include many side trips to well-known places that permit travelers to wander and ramble about to stop and rest in familiar surroundings. It also provides opportunities to wend one's way through places not quite so familiar.

"AARPer's Ferry" travels around the world. It scales high mountains and plunges to the depths of the oceans. It travels to space and beyond. Travelers can get on and off at their leisure without producing a boarding pass, a passport or a ticket. They are permitted to bring all the baggage they wish. There is no cost for handling.

This ferryboat carries a lifetime of memories plus a load of sanguinity, optimism, hope, faith and confidence in the future. It takes travelers to places that they will want to stay awhile and in some instances they may not want to leave. It must be said that the past is a great place to visit but I don't want to live there and I don't recommend that anyone live there.

This Time Machine is low tech and it doesn't cost any money to operate. No special crew is required. The only cost is time. This "AARPer's Ferry", this "Time Machine", is powered by the inexhaustible fuels of memory and reflection.

I'm A Geezer And I Thought I Would Be Smarter!

I thought that I would be smarter at this stage of my life. Not many people would use me as a lifeline on Who Wants to be a Millionaire? I don't even know how electricity works. It comes from the power plant through the wires, through the transformer and into the house. I plug in my drill, pull the trigger and it runs. How? I asked my son-in-law who is an engineer and he gave me a dissertation on how the current causes magnets to switch off and on in a circuit that makes the drill turn. Huh? How does the same current make the stove hot, the refrigerator cold, my razor cut whiskers and the dishwasher wash?

I don't know how a thermostat works. I know what a thermos is but what is a stat? I remember hearing doctors on "M*A*S*H" say stat that usually meant hurry. If I push the button one way the furnace comes on and warms the house. If I push it the other way the air conditioner comes on and cools the house. How does it know?

I don't understand how a TV works. People in New York City sing a song and someone else holds a device called a camera that sends an electronic signal through the wires to an antenna up to a satellite thousands of miles above the earth, back down to an antenna in Indy through a wire out to my house. I flip a switch, turn on my television set and see those people in my living room. I do know this. If someone painted a picture of those singers on a piece of wood and sent it through the UPS system to my house, I could look at it. That I understand.

I don't understand what happens when I place the ignition key in my car, turn it and the engine starts. Many years ago when I was helping Henry invent the Ford, I understood how a crank worked. How did that small key take the place of the crank?

I don't know who and why the first person ever thought to put an egg in a cake recipe. What does the egg do in there? I know what it does in a skillet and why it is there. I watched the Mythbusters program on TV recently and they put a raw egg in a car radiator and it stopped a substantial leak. Who thought of that?

I don't even know how to make ice cream. BW makes a liquid of milk, sugar, eggs, vanilla and other stuff and puts it in a metal can. I put the can inside a plastic bucket, put ice and salt around it and turn on the motor and it spins around and makes ice cream. I don't know how that happens. The ice [solid] becomes a liquid and the liquid becomes a semi-solid [ice cream]. How?

I don't even know how magnets work. I remember when many kids had the black and white Scottish terrier magnets. All we had was a real black and tan coonhound named Brownie. If you pushed them close together one way they stuck together; the other way and they repelled each other like the most popular girl in school rejects unworthy guys. How? Magnets are supposed to attract. Don't even talk to me about the North Pole and the South Pole and magnetic North.

I don't know why the holes in the electrical outlets are different sizes. Who thought of that? Every time I try to plug something in it never goes in the first time. What makes the difference?

There is no difference at all. Don't tell anyone but I am probably breaking several laws. I use my handy dandy file and make the big one the same size as the small one and that reduces my frustration level significantly. We have an old house and many of the receptacles are two holers and you know what that means! Every appliance and device manufactured since 1960 has three-pronged plug-ins. What to do? Either buy adapters or rummage around in the toolbox and find those side cutters and remove that obnoxious, pestiferous, useless third prong. I don't know why it is there any way.

I don't know how the magic box works. Go down to Sprawl-Mart and buy a box called a cooler but it doesn't cool anything. Put a warm can of Coca-Cola in it and leave it for two or three hours and it will be the same temperature as when you put it in there. If the box were a cooler the Coke would be colder. If not, why not? Put ice in the cooler and it melts so why is it called a cooler. BW uses our cooler to transport hot foods. Why isn't it called a hotter? So put cool items in and they remain cool longer. Put hot items in and they remain hot longer. How does it know the difference?

I truly thought I would be smarter by now but compared to Methuselah, I am still quite short in the tooth and I have time to learn more stuff.

The Sounds Of Grandma's House

Grandmothers are special. They let you play in the cabinets among their pots and pans. They let you help sew on the new sewing machine and if you should happen to throw the adjustments out of kilter they don't seem to care. You can play the piano as long and as loud as you like. If you should happen to break something they don't seem to mind as much as parents do.

I remember my Grandma Van who was a widow for many years. She lived in a small white house near Calvertville, Indiana, and I remember the sounds of her house. When I was a child growing up in the 1940s and 50s, life was quite different. Life was slower at least for me. Activities were different. People were more attached to a place and they didn't venture far from home. Don't be deluded, life was not easy. It never has been. Mayberry does not exist. People worked hard and diseases plagued them as they plague us -- some of the ones they contended with, no longer bother us. Interpersonal relationships were bothersome then as now. One aspect of life was much different then and that is sounds in the house.

The sounds in houses were different. Houses were much quieter. If one were to compare houses then to houses now, Grandma's house was a veritable mausoleum. Grandma did not have a washer and a dryer that hummed and growled and thumped through the laundry, unless you consider the sheets snapping on the solar-powered clothesline on a windy day. She did not have central heating with the rumbling furnace and the humming blower or central air conditioning with the grumbling compressor and the fan blowing cool air. She didn't have a microwave oven with its fan and electronic signal that dings when the popcorn is finished. She didn't have a television set that ran all day and night as background noise. She had no record player, CD player, boom box or other sound producing instruments. Neither did she have a freezer or an electric water pump. She didn't have a computer with clacking printer or annoying electronic games that reverberate throughout houses of today.   Her computer and printer were a pencil and a piece of paper. She didn't even have an inside toilet. There was a dearth of sounds in her house.

She had two sounds in her house though that I don't hear any more: a yellow singing canary and a ticking clock. Many people had those two items in their homes of yesteryear. If they were present in houses of today they could not be heard above the din.

Each day the canary would doff its top hat and cane, take its position center perch and sing and dance for her.   I made that up about the hat and cane. Grandma would talk to Buddy feed him and clean his cage. And for those amenities, Buddy entertained her and lessened the quietude of the day. I can still hear it chirping and tweeting. I don't remember the last time I saw a bird in someone's house.

Grandma also had a large clock that sat on the mantle. It tick-tocked through the day and night counting the minutes of life. It would also sound the alarm when it was time to arise for the day. As a child I sat in grandma's living room many Sunday afternoons and listened as the adults conversed. Interspersed with the words was the ticking of the clock. When a lull occurred, the clock kept on ticking. The same air that carried the words carried the ticking of the clock, the chimes on the quarter hour and the bonging on the hour. One other sound that I remember was the creaking sounds of Grandma's chair as she rocked.

How I wish that I could go back and sit in Grandma's lap and hear the singing canary and the ticking of the mantle clock. More than that, I wish I could hear her pleasant laughter and listen to her tell about the old days before the turn of the century -- the 20th century.

"We get 150 channels and there is nothing fit to watch."

Geezers Don't Do Extreme!

I am a Geezer. I don't do extreme unless it is to lower my cholesterol or my blood pressure. Is it just me or are Americans using the word **extreme** to the **extreme**? I wonder. It reminds me of the overuse of the words cool and awesome. If I hear those words once more I am going to take a hostage. It seems that every day another activity is described as extreme by the hyperbole machines that continually churn out information to entice spectators, viewers and consumers. Extreme! I have always thought that extreme meant just that, existing in a very high degree, being on the outside or going to great or exaggerated lengths; radical. The use of extreme is an undisguised effort to get the youthful and impressionable viewers and consumers to watch an event or to purchase a product or a service.

I even watched a promotion recently for a series of programs on Extreme History. What? Now that is something a Geezer might engage in. The program was a documentary on the history channel and it pertained to extreme engineering where difficult challenges were met. Another program described windmills in Holland as extreme inventions. There are programs describing and displaying extreme fashions. Clothing by designers for women who seek to expose more and more of their anatomy: arms, legs, ankles, knees, thighs, back, fronts, midriff, and behind. They show as much as possible and very soon they will be showing possible. They are extreme.

Extreme chess tournaments are conducted. I can hear the spectators now, "Here we go Geezers, here we go." "Get that checkmate, get that checkmate." "Take 'em to the Pawn shop, take 'em to the Pawn shop." A little obtuse humor clearly indicating that I am too hip for this room. It is obvious that I know very little about chess.

Extreme houses are touted and described as expensive, ostentatious, elaborate, multi-storied structures with pools and tennis courts. There is a television show called Extreme Makeover where clients visit a plastic surgeon who nips here and tucks there injects this and lifts that and makes Ugly Edna look like Beautiful Britney. Other programs remodel a house in ten days or restore a car to pristine condition.

Extreme sports are rampant. Athletes enter iron man competitions. They swim three miles, ride a bicycle for 112 miles and then run for 26 miles. Why? I am a geezer and geezers can't even run amuck. I have seen people with questionable intelligence trying to ride a skateboard down a banister. They fall and crumple with broken bones and other injuries too personal to mention. Skiers take a helicopter to the top of a mountain and then try to ski down with predictable results. And just yesterday I saw a guy trying to ride a mountain bicycle down a precipice where only skiers used to tread. Others dive off of rocks, buildings, bridges and other structures that result in numerous injuries and sometimes death. They are not brave or extreme they are obtuse and as thick through the head as a mule is across the rump! Just plain dumb.

Have you seen the rodeo event where four cowboys sit at a card table in a rodeo ring and a hostile bull is turned loose with them? The bull snorts, paws the ground and then charges at the four card players. He flings the table, chairs, cards and cowboys into the air like the tornado scene in the Wizard of Oz. The last cowboy to leave his seat is the winner. Frequently the bull makes bull paste out of them. I think those cowboys are selected from the white ribbon or honorable mention section of the breeding herd.

I have an extreme underarm deodorant produced by Right Guard. The company is shameless. They will do anything to sell the product to impressionable minds or those who fantasize about being great athletes or daredevils. Why do you think I have it? I perceive myself as being a daredevil. I have been known to ride the carousel with my granddaughter twice in one day. I am an extreme kind of guy. You can't stop me. That's what geezers do.

The roller coaster industry has been exploding exponentially in the past few years. Amusement parks have been trying to outdo all others in introducing greater thrills and lunch launching rides. Each spring and summer the airwaves are inundated with endless TV ads showing mostly prepubescent and pubescent riders screaming as they are propelled along the track of death. If I ride one of those you better hope that you are not behind me because I will be sharing my lunch with you.

I was listening to the car radio and my eardrums and sensibility were both shattered by the loud, raucous railings of an advertisement about an extreme annihilation monster truck rally. How can you exceed annihilation? Two announcers took turns screaming about the mammoth, colossal, gargantuan, fender-smashing, radiator bashing, gear grinding, smoke belching, brake squealing, tire crunching, rumbling, roaring, head banging trucks at the monster truck rally at the coliseum on Sunday. Bring the family and enjoy all the thrills and action at the extreme monster truck rally. When they finished I was so exhausted I had to stop the car and take a nap to recoup my energy. Geezers don't do monster truck rallies.

I have also noticed that the media uses the word extreme to target the young part of the population. I have not seen any advertisements for extreme Prescription H or extreme Hover Round races near the south rim of the Grand Canyon or for Liberty Mutual Life Insurance. I haven't seen any ads for extreme Denture Cream that won't let go even in a tornado. No extreme bingo games. Hold on there partner, maybe those have potential.

Please America. Everything is not extreme just as everything is not awesome or cool. Let me alone. I need some air.

The Wood Burning Stove Did it All

The kitchen is the nerve center of a household. I have many pleasant memories of my mother's kitchen when I was growing up. She spent much of her day in the kitchen preparing meals and cleaning afterward. Even today we spend quite a bit of time doing the same thing. Friends tend to cluster in the kitchen during holidays and other celebrations.

Our kitchen in metro-Calvertville was a place where the family gathered three times each day and ate hearty meals. If there were not five people around the table it meant that someone was ill or Dad was working a second job off the farm. When I was very short in the tooth, our kitchen was a sparsely furnished room in the back of the house. There were some cabinets and a countertop and sink with no running water and a table and chairs on one end with a walk-in pantry that housed the cream separator. There were two doorways one into the dining room and one to the outside. Beside the outside door was another small sink with a medicine cabinet on the wall. Beside the small sink was a huge wood burning Warm Morning Stove - kitchen range. It had a stovepipe that rose up about a meter and then turned 90 degrees into the chimney. That wood-burning stove did it all.

Mom's range had a black iron top with four lids that could be lifted out to access the firebox. The lazy "S" shaped tool was specially made to fit in a recess in the lid to lift it. On the back of the stove were two shelves. One was open and the other had a door that moved up and down similar to a garage door of today. They were used to store food items and keep them warm.

There were two doors on the front of the stove. One was to the firebox where wood and coal could be put into the grate. On the end of the grate was a place to attach the tool to shake the grate and let the ashes fall down into the ash pan. Of course the ash pan had to be emptied every day and wood had to be brought in. The other door was the oven. The doors and the front were covered with an enameled covering that made it look nice. That stove did it all.

The stove would boil, bake, fry and roast and serve as a heating pad to keep food warm. Mom prepared thousands of great meals on that stove. She would put milk on the back of the stove where it would fester and curdle and eventually become cottage cheese. Bread dough had a permanent parking place on the stove. The stove heated the flat irons. We did not have electricity or gas on the farm or microwave ovens. Gadzooks! How did we survive?

A water reservoir with an enamel coated lid was on the far right side where mom heated water. It would hold a gallon or two and it would get hot enough to scald a chicken. In the morning Dad would get his shaving water out of it. We also kept a teakettle on top of the stove. It would become so crusted with lime that it weighed more than Orson Wells. Our water was harder than a banker's heart during the depression. On wash day the copper boiler was placed on top of the stove to heat laundry water.

It was also a human warmer. I remember bursting into the house as cold as a polar bear's nose and standing close to the stove to get warm. Wet gloves and hats were placed on and in the stove to dry. We would open the oven door and place our stocking covered frigid feet on it to warm them. It also was supplemental heat for the rest of the house. Long after we got electricity mom kept the stove because it kept the kitchen warm.

The stove was an integral part of our health plan. When I got a bad cold, I don't remember ever having a good cold, the stove came to the rescue again. Just before I went to bed, Dad would slather Vicks Salve on my neck. Then he would wrap a towel or cloth around the stovepipe until it was one nanosecond from bursting into flame and then swathe it around my neck and whisk me off to bed. I can still feel the hot cloth and smell the Vicks.

Last night the temperature got down to single digits at our house. This morning I wish that I could stand beside mom's stove and get warm and then reach into the oven and get a freshly baked biscuit.

Winter In Yesteryear

There is a person in my life who shall remain nameless who maintains, no ~~she~~ that person will argue vehemently, that the snow was always deeper back then and it was colder back then. I counter that the weather bureau records would not support ~~her~~ that claim. But I never win the argument. That causes me to write some anecdotage of winters past.

Winters used to be colder than a landlord's heart when the rent is due. In the Good Old Days snow would be deeper than Albert Einstein. [A bit of cerebral humor for you] The countryside would be as white and still as fallen cumulus clouds. I often thought that it looked like someone had sprinkled powdered sugar all over the countryside. The temperature would always get down around Bedford as the wags would say around the potbellied stove in the Calvertville Store. What they were trying to say was that it would get really cold; the temperature would be low. If you have to explain a metaphor it loses some of its power.

Horses and cattle would snort and stomp and their breath reminded me of a steam locomotive going down the track with steam billowing along the side. They always found the South side of the barn and stood in the sunshine on winter days.

We always made snowmen -- never snow women. We rolled the balls of snow as large as we could lift and stacked them forming the body just as people do today. Then we got an old hat from the barn or shed and used coal or stones for eyes and buttons on his coat. A stick served as the mouth and a larger one became a staff. And of course a larger stick served as a pipe or cigar. Sometimes we put a shovel or pitchfork in his hand and an old rag or scarf around his neck. Frosty then stood staring at the world until he had a meltdown. BW just said that kids today don't make snowmen. They cocoon inside the house and make virtual ones instead. I noticed that she hasn't made any this winter either.

Icicles always fascinated me. I have noted over the past many years that I do not see as many icicles as when I was a kid. Back then houses were not insulated or if they were it was not very well. Heat escaped through the walls and ceilings through the attic and melted the snow and ice on the roof. The sun would contribute to the meltage as well. The result was huge stalactite icicles that formed on eaves. They made wonderful though ineffective swords to fight the Sheriff of Nottingham or to sail the Seven Seas as a pirate fighting for treasure. They would shatter at the first thrust but replacements were easy.

Kids and adults frequently ate icicles as a non-fat, no cholesterol, no calorie and no taste Popsicle. Sometimes adults, on a whim, would stir hot tea or coffee with them to cool the liquid lava. They looked so pure and clear and irresistible. They sparkled like elongated diamonds. But, when I think of all the soot and dirt that was in snow and on rooftops that was imbedded in the icicle I wonder how we survived.

Mom's kitchen was the warmest place on the planet. We tended to play outside until we became walking icebergs. Then we would roar into the kitchen to get warm. We would pile our coats, gloves and sometime socks on or as close to the stove as possible to dry them. Sometimes the oven was pressed into service as a dryer. We never heard of a dryer.

Fingers and toes felt toasty when we put them on again. Mom always had something good to eat or drink to chase the chill.

We had a huge wood-burning stove in our kitchen. We also burned coal in it later on. It was mostly black with some chrome like trim. The stovepipe came out of the back and made a 90-degree turn into the chimney. The top had four lids that could be lifted so wood could be placed into the burning chamber. The chamber could also be accessed from the front. Ashes were shaken down through the grate and removed in a pan located in the front which was much like a drawer of today. The oven was heated by the same fire as the top. There was a reservoir to heat water on the right side of the top. An enclosed metallic box was located above the top to keep food warm. There was a third level shelf where pots, pans and other things were stored. We ate many excellent meals prepared on that old iron beast. It also kept that end of the house quite warm.

As I write this on Sunday, February 23, 2003, we are experiencing a winter wonderland of snow here in Avon. More is predicted tonight. Aarrrrrgh. As much as I like snow, I don't know how much more I can take.

Thoughts While Sitting on The Porch at The Calvertville Store

The other day I went back to the Calvertville Store. It was quick and easy because I went in my mind. The shade of the porch felt good as I opened the screen door with the silk-screened Colonial Bread ad on it and strolled inside. Ralph smiled and said, "Boy, it has been a long time since I saw you. How you been?"

"I have been doing fine, how about yourself?" I said as I plunged my hand into the cold water of the Coca-Cola cooler. Feeling around I pulled out a six-ounce Coca Cola in the familiar green bottle. "Ralph, how about a bag of salted peanuts?" .

"Sure thing, that will be ten cents for the peanuts and the pop."

"Thanks, Ralph," I said and went out on the porch to sit a spell on a nail keg. I poured the peanuts into the bottle and thought about life as I enjoyed that wonder elixir.

We are right smack dab in the middle of another presidential election and that caused me to wonder. I have been aware of presidential elections since the middle of the last century and they all sound alike anymore. I am so old that I remember Preparation "G". The presidential wannabe brutalizes the incumbent with his record. The incumbent beats the wannabe over the head with the club of reality and calls him a liar. Why does every candidate promise to cut spending and waste yet the national debt goes up faster than Superman chasing an errant asteroid?

I reflected about all the sick people I know. People all over the world pray for the sick to be well. So do I. What would happen if all people were suddenly well and if no one needed to take medicine? The world economy would collapse like a cheap tent in a summer storm. Ponder that.

Think about all of the people employed in the field of medicine. There are doctors, nurses, administrators in hospitals as well as the support staff of food service, housekeeping, and maintenance and don't forget the EMTs and the companies that make the medical trucks and supplies. How about the sales people in the medical arena? Don't forget Lilly and all the companies that develop and sell drugs. How about the insurance companies that sell medical insurance and the lawyers who file cases and the court system that is bogged down with cases on malpractice suits. I almost forgot the nursing homes and all the employees there and the local drug store. Don't forget the family doctor and her staff and the medical specialists who exist just beyond the headlights of the family doctor. How about the companies that make and sell medical equipment? Could we afford to be well? I wonder.

Then I contemplated about the alcohol and other drug problems that plague America and the world. I am cynical. The war on drugs and alcohol will not be won until the reasons that cause people to want them are found and addressed. I have noticed that those who try to drown their troubles in alcohol learn that troubles can swim. Those who try to escape life through other drugs find out that troubles find them because they always leave a forwarding address. It is as easy to get illegal drugs in America as it is to get into a community college.

I am puzzled by tattoos. Back in the middle of the last century I served in the Navy under the command of Captain John Paul Jones. A little Navy humor there. The only people who had tattoos were in the Navy or had been or had survived the Nazi death camps of W.W. II. Now a great many people have a tattoo somewhere on their body and that caused me to wonder. If tattoos are so beautiful and allow people to express themselves, why don't the wearers put them on their faces ala Mike Tyson? Now that I think about it, that is a perfect example of why they don't.

I took another drink, swatted a fly and thought about the economy in Indiana and America. I pondered why so many plants are closing and jobs are being shipped to Mexico, the Pacific Rim and India. Why can't boards of directors and CEOs understand that they are cutting the throat of the American Economy? Are you with me? However, if you are wearing a shirt made in Columbia, watch a TV made in Korea, use a computer made in Japan, take medicine made in Ireland, use a water heater made in Mexico, buy tools made in China, wear cologne from France, eat fruit grown in Chili and green beans grown in Guatemala, take pictures with a camera made in Taiwan, add oil to your car from the Mid-East, drive a car from Germany, dust American souvenirs made in China, plan to use Christmas decorations made in Austria and eat chocolate made in Switzerland, don't complain about jobs going overseas. We often shoot ourselves in the foot with an Israeli made Uzi.

It is amazing what comes to mind while sitting on the porch at the Calvertville Store.

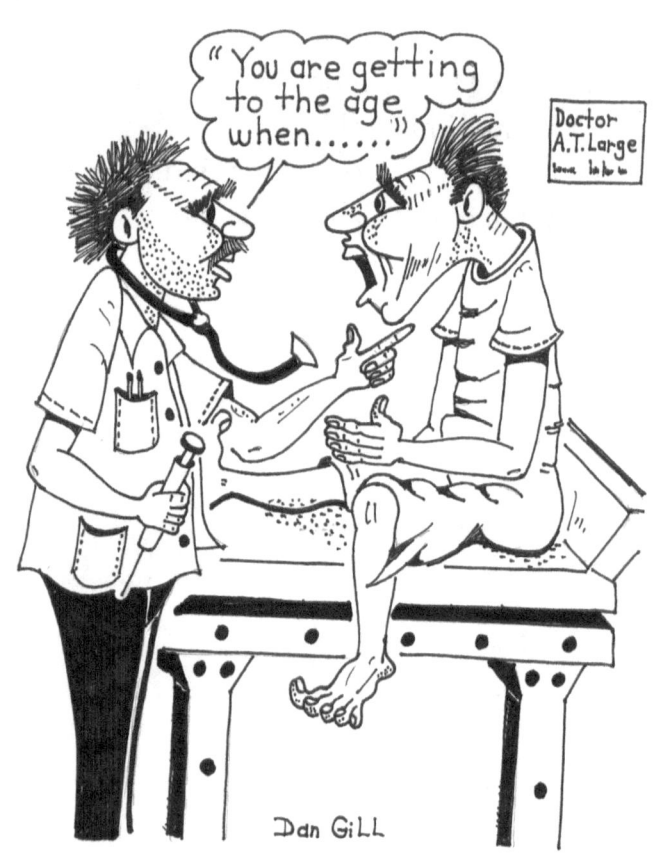

The Times They Are Achangin' For Geezers Too

Way back in the 60s, that would be the 1960s, Bob Dylan sang a song about how times were changing. I was a young sprout then and it didn't apply much to me then but lately I have noticed that things are changing in my world. I have noticed that as the years go by, everything seems uphill from where I am? Stairs are steeper, groceries are heavier, and everything is farther away. Yesterday I walked to the corner and I was horrified to discover how long our street had become!

People are less considerate now, especially the young ones. They speak in whispers all the time! If you ask them to speak up they just keep repeating themselves, endlessly mouthing the same silent message until they're red in the face! Do they think I am a lip reader?

I also have a feeling that these people are much younger than I was at the same age. On the other hand, something has been making people who used to be my own age so much older than I am. I ran into an old friend the other day and she has aged so much that she didn't even recognize me. I got to thinking about the poor dear while I was shaving this morning, and in doing so, I glanced at my own reflection. I noticed that even mirrors are not made the way they used to be!

Clothing manufacturers are part of the conspiracy too! Why else would they suddenly start labeling a size 38 pair of pants as 42 or 44? Do they think no one notices that these things no longer fit around the waist?

Another thing, everyone drives so fast today! You're risking life and limb if you just happen to pull onto the freeway in front of them. All I can say is, their brakes must wear out extremely quick, the way I see them screech and swerve in my rear view mirror.

The people who make bathroom scales are in on it as well. Do they think I actually believe the number I see on that dial? Hah! I would never let myself weigh that much! Just whom do these people think they're fooling?

I'd like to call up someone in authority to report what's going on – but the telephone company is in on the conspiracy too: they've printed the phone books in such small type that no one could ever find a number in there!

Dylan was right, the times they are achangin'.

She Did Not Know Captain Kangaroo

I don't know how much more I can take. Lately my self-esteem, self-image and fragile psyche have been bludgeoned into submission by the cudgel of reality. My self-image has been made so small that I could walk fully erect under a snail trail. My psyche has been so diminished that I now can play handball on the curb in front of our house and we don't even have a curb. My self-esteem is as insignificant as a dust bunny under the dresser in the back bedroom beneath the stairs covered by a tarpaulin in the guesthouse of a long dead Gold Rush shanty in a ghost town in Southern Nevada that was shattered by atomic testing in 1943.

BW and I along with some friends were eating in a restaurant on Indy's West Side. Our server was a friendly, young lady. You can't say waitress any more because it is not politically correct. She was wearing an apron that had several large pockets on the front and sides in which she carried bottles of various condiments and ancillary items. It seemed to be quite handy and efficient. I remarked, "You have more pockets in your apron than Captain Kangaroo had in his jacket."

She looked at me and grew puzzled. Her forehead looked like corduroy and she said, "Captain Who?"

Well imagine my surprise. My "sixhead", some of us don't have as much hair as we once had, furrowed and I sank down in my chair, pleading, "Captain Kangaroo. He had a television show for children that ran for nearly thirty years. Mr. Green Jeans, the Bunny Rabbit and the Clock were all on the show."

She smiled benignly and said, "I never heard of him or his show." It quickly became apparent that she was culturally deprived. I could tell just by looking at her. But that is not the end of the story. There is more.

BW and I had a holiday party at our house. We were playing Family Feud. Admittedly it was the first edition but it was manufactured in the late 70s - 1970 not 1870. One question asked for cast names of the huge western TV show "Gunsmoke". You know who I am talking about - Matt Dillon, Chester Good, Kitty Russell, Doc Adams, Festus Hagen, Newly, Ma Smalley, Moss Gremick and others. Three people in the group of ten had never heard of "Gunsmoke". They had never seen it and knew nothing about it. It gets worse.

BW and I were talking and wondering if Staples might still sell carbon paper. How many people today have used carbon paper? A young office worker of today never uses it and probably has never used a typewriter. I go on.

I was getting a rental car at a local repair shop. We have had six accidents since we moved to the metro area. Not one of these incidents was our fault. The young woman who represented Enterprise Rental Cars talked me through the form and asked for my signature. Then she asked that I initial four other places to indicate that she had explained other options or that I had rejected or accepted portions of the deal. I remarked, "This sounds like Radar on "M*A*S*H" when he had Col. Blake initial that he had signed and signed that he had initialed various army forms. She looked puzzled. I continued, "You know Corporal Radar O'Reilly. The company clerk.

He was from Ottuma, Iowa. He was short and wore glasses and slept with a Teddy Bear." I could tell by her lack of expression that she was blissfully unaware of who Radar was.

There were three people in the office at the time - two women who were 20 something and a man who was early 30 something. None of them knew who Radar was or had ever watched the TV show M*A*S*H. I slumped in despair. There was some vindication later.

When I returned the rental car there were four people in the office area. Three were different and one who was there during the previous conversation. I politely mentioned the conversation about "M*A*S*H". This time the three new people had all heard of the show and knew Radar. What a relief. I thought I was in the Twilight Zone.

I can just hear someone ask, "What do you mean the Twilight Zone?" That is another story. Move over Methuselah and Rod Serling. I have to sit down.

I Ain't Never Heerd of Sich a Thing!

Audrey alert. I feel compelled to warn readers that the subject of this story is about the sweetest, cutest, most progressive baby ever born. Well, she is at least in the top three of all time. That would be Audrey Grace our first grandchild. A visit to Audreyville takes me back thirty plus years when our two girls (TW and TM) were babies. It is a time warp. What a difference.

Audrey is eating cereal, meat and vegetables. As a typical baby sometimes more goes on the outside than the inside. TM and Todd have a spoon that looks like there is dried cake batter on the bowl. It is pink and when it is dipped in the vegetables it will turn white if the food is too hot. Our girls ate out of metal spoons just like everyone else. If they spit it out and squawked we figured it must be too hot. We did have a rubber one that smelled like a horse's breath after the first month of use.

When Audrey goes on a trip in the car, she is strapped into a capsule of plastic and padding that rivals an astronaut suit. The hospital had to approve the seat before Audrey could be dismissed. It is equipped with seat belts, padded all around then covered with a hood and blankets. Then the seat is fastened to hooks attached to the frame of the car and strapped in the back seat facing backwards. She would survive a direct hit by a Scud missile.

We had a seat that was made of a piece of canvas attached to two metal hooks that hung in the middle of the front seat of the car between BW and me. It had a plastic steering wheel attached to it. TW and TM would have exited through the windshield on impact.

Audrey sits in a Space Age high chair on rollers that lock. The feet are spread-eagled like a giraffe trying to drink from a pond. It is constructed of technologically inspired and computer designed plastic and padding. There is a saddle horn, called a safety cone, protruding up from the front of the seat to keep her from sliding out. It also has a seatbelt to keep her from squirting out of the chair like a seed from the mouth of Toothless Cal at the County Fair watermelon-eating contest. It is almost large enough for me to sit in. She looks like a Chipmunk sitting in the bed of a dump trunk.

At mealtime we set our girls on top of an old wooden orange crate that was nailed to a tomato crate that leaned at an angle like the Leaning Tower of Pisa. We hooked their diapers between the slats to keep them from falling off. It is difficult to scoot on rough sawed slats so they didn't move very much.

When Audrey gets new clothing it must be washed before she can wear it. Clothing from the best stores must be washed and ironed before the skin of "Her Grace" touches it. Her mother said it was because of germs and chemicals used in the manufacturing process. Of course today most clothing is made in Bangladesh, China and Taiwan.

BW made most of our daughters' clothing for years. She could whip out a dress in no time from a 25-cent remnant from the fabric store. We swapped clothing among friends and relatives in a never-ending sharing frenzy. We never thought of those things. We picked up clothes from yard sales, dumpsters and found along the road and the girls wore them home that day.

Audrey has never had a cloth diaper on her leaking and spewing parts. There are two New Albany area landfills that have been crammed full of disposable diapers and closed since June 14. They have baby-wipes, spray on oil, oceans of lotions, Velcro fasteners and a Diaper Genie for used seat covers so that you never smell or tell they are around. Audrey has no concept of diaper rash. So antiseptic.

We used cloth diapers with dull pins that you had to run through your hair to make them slick enough to penetrate the cloth. We rinsed out the dirty ones in the commode and kept both kinds in a diaper pail until washing. The odoriferous emanations from that container could be used in chemical warfare. Our girls often developed a rash that made them look like they had a tookas sunburn.

How times have changed. I knew Stella 35 years ago when she was 85 years old. She was overwhelmed by the advancements in her world. She would say "Well, I jest ain't never heerd of sich a thing!" Stella, neither have I.

What Was Your Favorite Fast Food?

One day our granddaughter Audrey will ask, "Grandpa, what was your favorite fast food when you were growing up?" Then I will have to 'fess up and say, "We didn't have fast food when I was growing up." To those of you who are still learning, the industry prefers to say Quick Serve food.

"Oh Grandpa," she will say with a twinkle in her eye, "quit kidding around. Where did you eat?"

"We ate at home, we all sat down together at the table and I had two options: Take it or leave it."

By this time she will probably be rolling her eyes and laughing so hard she won't be able to stand up. Then I'll scrape the moss off of the north side of my body and put a dollop of Cornhuskers Lotion behind my ears that at one time were wet but now are as parched as the deepest part of Death Valley.

There are a few other things about my childhood growing up in Highland Township that will be ancient to her and perhaps beyond her ability to believe.

My parents never wore Levi jeans or any other Levi product. Levi's were being produced but they were not popular in our area at that time. Neither of my parents ever stepped on a golf course to play the game or to hunt mushrooms. Amazing. My parents never went to a health club to exercise or to Jazzercise or any other "cise." They worked too hard and long to have any energy for such.

My grandparents never traveled out of the county in my kidhood. My parents seldom did. My parents were only in debt for about four years from 1941-1945 when they were paying off the mortgage on the farm. After that they never owed anyone or incurred any debt of any kind. They married in 1934 in the depths of the Great Depression and that experience caused them to never be in debt for fear they could not pay or they would lose the farm. They had one credit card once but never used it. Their credo was "If you don't have the money, you don't need it."

My parents never drove me to soccer practice. None of us ever heard about soccer except during a fight between siblings when one might yell, "Sock her!" They never drove me to Little League Baseball games. The kids on the farms around us played what townies called sandlot baseball. In our vernacular it was called hay field or cow pasture baseball. When I was in junior high and early high school team member parents shared transportation when some of us started playing basketball. Then, I acquired a car and that ended.

In my kidhood outdoor sports consisted of baseball games, swimming in the creek, snowball fights, building forts, making snowmen and sliding down the hill on a sled or a piece of galvanized roofing. We rode bicycles over gravel roads, played basketball on the barnyard court, Cowboys and Indians and army with the Crody boys over in Kelly Bend. There was never any organization, no parent support group, no leagues or travel squads, no printed rulebook, no trophies or uniforms. It was the greatest form of democracy because everyone had to agree on the rules and take turns. There was no commissioner to settle disagreements.

I did not walk to school ten miles in the snow uphill both ways. We rode the school bus that stopped at the end of our lane which was approximately the length of three or four football fields. It was cold and wet getting from the bus to the house and vice versa.

We never had television until I was in Junior High School. No one ever heard of a computer or the Internet. I never tasted pizza until I went to college. I never had a telephone in my room. Our only phone was a wall-mounted box that was a party line. You had to go through the operator, Edith Buckner, to call out of the neighborhood. Our newspaper was delivered on R.R. 1, by Clyde Flory, the mailman, who put it in the mailbox at the end of the lane.

I never saw the Lone Ranger or Roy Rogers or anyone else actually kill someone. They would shoot the gun out of Black Bart's hand. No blood, no violence. The doctor actually came to the house when you were sick. Drugs were purchased at the drugstore.

I never sassed my parents. Well I did once and then dad and I had a meeting with the "Hickory Board of Education" and that never happened again. Parents actually disciplined their children and expected them to mind. Well, most of them did as they do today.

How did we survive?

"If you have ever taken a catalog to Ft. Necessity and didn't order anything, you may be a geezer."

Movies are not real life!

BW and I went to a movie during the Christmas Season: We saw "Christmas with the Kranks" from a book written by John Grisham. He is branching out from his usual legal genre. As movies go it was rather good. It was a thoroughly implausible story but it was entertaining. At least there was no nudity, no sexual acts implied or displayed, no vulgarities or profanities, no defiance of authority, no destruction of property or police chases with guns blasting everything in sight and no large explosions with a huge ball of fire in the background. It seems that those are standard fare for movies today. For those reasons we don't see many movies because those who make movies have forgotten about us and those like us. This movie had a heart-warming ending and brought a tear to many an eye.

Sitting there in a plush theater with surround sound I mused about the fact that no one ever told me when I was a kid that movies were not real. I grew up thinking that what I saw on Saturday afternoon was real and that it did happen just that way. Roy Rogers and Gene Autry were my heroes and could do no wrong. They could see the problem, find the bad guys, engage them in a gun battle and send them off to jail. All within about 30 to 45 minutes. **[Back then the bad guys always wore black hats until Hopalong Cassidy came along and thought outside of the box. He was a good guy but he wore a black hat and black outfit.]**

If any of the good guys were ever wounded it was a flesh wound in the shoulder and never the shoulder of their gun hand. Or, sometimes they got a nick on the head that was not serious. Some of the bad guys were killed but it was not gruesome or with blood splattering over seven counties like today. Now I am going to tell the truth. I had a suspicion that movies were not real in the same way I thought about the jolly fat man with the long white beard who travels in December who shall remain nameless in case he reads this book.

You cannot depend on Hollywood for your knowledge of history. Hollywood never lets the truth get in the way of telling a good story. If it pleases the court let me present a prime exhibit to support this allegation. Exhibit 'A' is the movie Fahrenheit 9/11 that Michael Moore released recently about the Bush Administration and anything even randomly related to Bush. The timing was perfect as it was released, or did it escape, during the election year. I recommend that you get a huge saltshaker and sprinkle its contents generously on that "Mockumentary" as you ingest it and try to digest it. Exhibit 'B' would be the movie that Oliver Stone produced about the assassination of JFK a few years ago. End of rant.

Movies are fantasy and nothing more. They are instruments to help the viewer escape from the reality of day-to-day living. No one and I mean no one would go to a movie about your life and where you work. Lawyers, policemen and educators all say TV and movies about their work are not real. Movies are legal devices used to extend a hand into your pocket to extract money and use it in lavish living. Why else can Hollywood pay actors such as Tom Cruise, Julia Roberts and Leonardo DiCaprio

$20 million to play in a movie? Only because you and I are willing to pay the ticket price and patronize their advertisers.

BW and I stepped up to the ticket window and she out shuffled me so I had to pay. A teenage type young lady smiled widely and politely asked, "May I help you?" I said, "Yes, I would like two adult tickets, adjusted for senior citizens and matinee prices." [We attended the 11:00 a.m. showing on Saturday.] She replied, "That will be $12.00 please." I said, "Twelve Dollars! I remember when we were dating that we could go to a double feature movie, see a cartoon, a short subject and previews for a buck fifty." She smiled weakly, rolled her eyes while glancing at an equally young male ticket seller beside her and smoozed, "I am sorry, but our ticket prices went up recently and during the holidays, senior citizen discounts and matinee prices are frequently not in effect." I got eight dollars back from my twenty. She smiled as she gave me the ticket and said, "Thank you, enjoy the movie and come again." What a nice person. She still charged me too much. Don't get me started on the price of popcorn and sodas at the theater.

Geezers quit trying to hold their stomachs
in no matter who walks into the room.

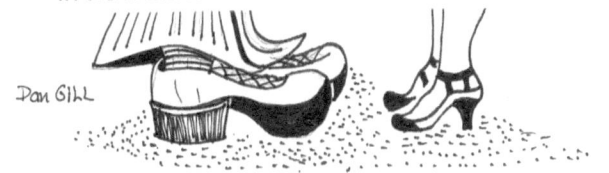

Don Gill

As Time Goes By - Part 1

Rod Serling introduced many episodes of The Twilight Zone by saying, "Picture this, if you will"... a small town in middle America, in South Central Indiana in the middle of the last century. Worthington, Indiana, to be exact. The time May. The year 1956. The latest crop of high school graduates was being thrust out into the world to seek their fortunes. I was in that group of pilgrims launched on the sea of uncertainty in our own Mayflower seeking the new world. We knew it was out there and we were off to find it and conquer it.

Twenty-three bright-eyed graduates were planning to set the world on fire. Sadly somewhere along the way someone either stole our matches or dipped them in the waters of defeat. We were going to grab the brass ring and win a free ride on the merry-go-round of life. However, when some came around an insidious force moved the rings back and their arms were not long enough to reach them. We were so naïve that we thought Betty Jo's Flower Garden would always be there to sell flowers and plants. That Hobart and Dimple would always greet us in the Worthington State Bank and help with our financial needs. Don Wilson would always smile and ask to "Fill 'er up" at the Standard Station.

If we needed some candy, notions or gifts we knew that Tresslar's Five and Dime would be at the ready to fill our needs. Harold Skeel at The Rexall Drug Store would quickly and efficiently fill our prescriptions that the doctors Moses would write and we could always buy the Sunday Paper there on a hot summer Sunday morning. Some of us were patients of the doctors Moses and we counted on them to keep us healthy. Many were also the patients of Dr. Fender who likewise knew just what to do to diagnose and treat our aches and pains.

We just knew that the high school would always be there on Main Street and "Wheezer" and "Doc" would be in charge. The State Theater operated by "Red" was our escape hatch to other worlds and we hoped that it would remain so. If we needed anything in the hardware line we knew that Lloyd Rollison would have it. If he didn't have it we didn't need it.

We just knew if we ever needed a haircut Bill Dixon would stand at the ready with sharpened scissors and talcum powder. The Busy Bee was going to continue forever to serve burgers, fries and milkshakes along with the Triangle and the Highway 67 café. The Marathon Inn anchored the north side of town and we thought we could depend on it to remain there for a couple of millennia.

Lloyd Stahl and B.B. Mitten would sell insurance as long as we or anyone needed it. Alva Cooksey, Bob Carter, Wilson Short, Bob Terrell, Doc Pickard and Otto Baker would always be there to sell gasoline, fix flats and repair our cars. The Star Electric would always provide our electrical needs.

We thought Clovis would be there to sell us a new car and Garvin Mitchel and Bob Ferris would sell us farm equipment and that Herbert

Sloan would always sell seed corn and run the seed house. If we ever needed a cow shipped to market Wilson Baker would be the one to call.

We just knew that the Worthington Times would forever be the eyes and ears of the community. Little did we know how the town would change as time goes by. None of the merchants or businesses listed above remain in service to the community. Most of the people have passed over the great divide and live only in memory.

Who Will Watch The Home Place?

People were meandering through the parks and down the paths of falling leaves. It was one of those days in the fall when the sun shines brighter than a five-year old child's face on Christmas morning. The leaves were rustling down in a cascade of red, yellow and brown. The temperature felt like warm bath water and just as comfortable. Squirrels were rushing around storing nuts for the long winter that was coming. Long lines of geese were flying south in a V-necked sweater formation. Farmers were busy in the fields harvesting the last of the soybeans and getting a good start on the corn. The cattle and horses were fatter and their coats were thicker as they prepared for a confrontation with Jack Frost and Deep Freeze.

Down the road the fall high school teams, football, cross country and volleyball, were practicing for the coming contests while the band rehearsed for the fall marching season. Laughing elementary children were playing at recess in the bright amarillo colored sunshine. Local merchants and civic organizations were preparing for the annual Fall Festival to entice weekend travelers to spend their money.

Today, though, my mind takes me back to the place where I was born and raised and the community that has changed so dramatically that I hardly recognize it. I remember that we had a workshop or tool shed where dad kept many of his tools. There was a thick rough-hewn workbench of soft wood probably poplar or pine. My brother and I would practice to see how many hits it took to drive a nail into the bench. You were a man when it took only one. Of course the length or penny of the nail made a difference. Why are nail sizes expressed in penny?

I remember specific tools Dad used almost daily in his work as farmer and carpenter. We had a Bloomfield jack that we used for a hundred years to lift almost anything we could get the jack under or get a chain around. The Harrah Manufacturing Company in Bloomfield, Indiana, made the jack.

Dad had a crosscut saw that we used to cut wood every winter. He would be on one end and Brother and I would work the other end. At times we felt like flags flapping in the wind as he whipped the saw back and forth across the log. He had a wooden toolbox that he had used early in his life to carry his carpenter tools. Later he gave it to me and I proudly keep it on my workbench. I can still see his hammers, axe, crowbar, mattock, handsaws, brace and bit, sledgehammer and square. He used those tools to earn a living and to keep the place in good repair. Today his workbench is empty and strewn with miscellaneous articles of no worth. His tools have been sold or given to relatives. It saddens me to see his workspace in such a state of disrepair.

There's a lovely green meadow and field where we once put up hay. There is a wetland area and a clear-running stream that flows from it. As boys my brother and I swam in that stream and waded through the water early in the spring before the water was warm enough to swim. Our ducks laid green eggs on the banks that we sold. There is something therapeutic about running streams that sooth troubled brows and ease the aches and pains of life. How I loved the freedom of roaming about the home place with the wind and the rain in my face. It was my anchor and bedrock of security; a shield from fear and want. Memories flit around me like butterflies in the summer sun as I walk about the old place today. Thoughts swirl about my feet like beautiful leaves blown by a sudden October breeze

My mother spent the last 18 months of her life in a nursing home suffering from Alzheimer's disease. She slowly sank into a dark abyss where we couldn't find her. I am not sure she recognized me as her youngest son born to her when she was just 23 years old. She did smile and laugh and make witty comments, which gave me indication that her mind still functioned at some level. Out of the blue one day as I was trying to converse with her she asked, "How are things over at the Farm?" She and dad bought the farm in 1941. He slowly slipped away from us eight years before as the weight of 89 years and a life of duty pulled him from our grasp. They were married for over 63 years and lived on the farm for nigh on to fifty years as they say in Calvertville. She lived there for six more years after he passed away.

When she asked that question tears came to my eyes as I remembered the words of an old bluegrass song: "Who will watch the home place, who will tend my hearts dear space, who will fill my empty place, when I am gone from here?"

As Time Goes By - Part Two

The year 1956 was a major milestone in my life. It is one of the major steps of life that all go through on the road to becoming an adult. I am on a roll with that magical year 1956. So bear with me for a few more words on the subject.

It was a good year. You could go down to the dealership and buy a brand new Ford car for as little as $1,748 or as much as $3,150. A new house cost about $22,000 or what a lot costs today. Clyde Flory, our mailman on R.R. 1, was selling postage stamp for 3 cents. Bob Carter sold gasoline all day for 23 cents per gallon and sometimes on special five gallons for a dollar. Bob and Gayle had milk for 97 cents a gallon and a loaf of bread for 18 cents. Borders IGA had chuck roast for sale every day at about 35 cents per pound and spare ribs for 39 cents a pound. Cabbage was available at Soliday's store for 4 cents per pound and eggs were 45 cents per dozen. Moore Brothers, the former Mexico store, offered coffee for 69 cents a pound and Kool-Aid was 5 cents a package. Ollie Flory had Life Savers for 5 cents.

All of you are thinking that you wish prices were still that low. However, reality will slap you in the face with a dead Mackerel when you realize that the average household annual income was $4,450 dollars or about $85 dollars per week. How does that sound? People today spend more than that on cable in some areas and Internet access.

I remember "Gunsmoke" with James Arness on TV. Game shows were big with "The $64,000 Challenge", "Twenty-One", "Tic Tac Dough" and "The Price is Right" which has outlived all of them. "As The World Turns" and "The Edge of Night" ruled the soaps. Huntley and Brinkley began a long run on the NBC nightly news.

Elvis made his debut on "The Ed Sullivan Show" with the memorable view from the waist up. He made his first movie, "Love Me Tender", and "Heartbreak Hotel" and "Hound Dog" were huge hits for him. "The Honeymooners" starring Jackie Gleason was a hit along with "I Love Lucy", "General Electric Theater", "December Bride", "The Perry Como Show" and "The Jack Benny Show."

Movies that year included James Dean in "Giant", his last movie, with Elizabeth Taylor and Rock Hudson. "Around the World in 80 Days" was the monster hit that year. Others were "The King and I", "Friendly Persuasion", "The 10 Commandments", "Bus Stop" and "The Searchers" starring my all time hero John Wayne.

The U.S. tested the hydrogen bomb and tensions rose dramatically between Israel and its Arab neighbors. Sounds familiar. The luxury liner Andrea Doria was rammed by the Stockholm in heavy fog. The Doria sank with the loss of 52 lives but 1,662 were saved. Ringling Brothers Circus quit their tent shows in favor of arenas. They are in town in September. BW and I will be there.

Singers of great renown that year included Pat Boone, Johnny Cash, Perry Como, Bill Haley and the Comets, Elvis and Dean Martin. Many feet adorned with bobby sox danced to their music.

Saturday night prime time was huge: "The Lawrence Welk Show", "Masquerade Party", "Beat the Clock" and "The Buccaneers."

Don't forget "Oh, Susanna", "Hey Jeannie", "High Finance", "Gunsmoke", "The Jackie Gleason Show" and "People are Funny." Also showing were "The Perry Como Show", "Caesar's Hour", "The George Gobel Show" and "Your Hit Parade."

New products on the market included Midas Mufflers, Raid, Yahtzee, Jif Peanut Butter and Tupperware.

Those were the days my friend, I thought they'd never end. Geezers remember those days.

Black and White
- An ode to times long gone

I remember back in the early days of television in Indiana. We lived on the farm in the country. At the time we had heard that television was a reality. Now you could have walking, talking movies and shows in your home. No more need to go to the cinema.

We did not have a television set at that time so we, the ever enterprising and adventuresome sort, visited neighbors and relatives and watched some special events. I remember going to visit John Burr Calvert who, appropriately lived on the near eastside of downtown Calvertville, to watch the Friday night fights on his black and white set. Gillette sponsored them. We sat there with some of his grandchildren and others and watched the likes of Kid Gavilan whose specialty was the bolo punch that he supposedly learned while cutting sugar cane in Cuba. Bet me. He was probably from Des Moines, Iowa. We also watched Chuck Davies, Ezzard Charles, Sugar Ray Robinson, Rocky Graziano and Rocky Marciano. We also went to Bert and Grace Davis' house and watched a state championship basketball game and sometimes the New Year's Day Parade. One time the horizontal hold was not functioning so we watched zig zag lines for a time and listened. None of us knew how to adjust the knob for such problems.

Out in the country people purchased an antenna and placed it on the top of a tall pole to attract the over the air signals from Bloomington and Indianapolis, the only sources for TV back then.

Then one day, "Saints preserve us, glory be and joy to the world all the boys and girls now", dad and mom bought a black and white Muntz TV. I believe that it was manufactured by Sarkes-Tarzian, Inc., in Bloomington. If not it should have been. We plugged it in and with great anticipation waited while the tubes warmed up so it could work. And there on our own TV set we could watch it snow with the best of them.

We gathered around that small set like baby piglets nuzzling up to their momma hoping for sustenance. From that day until now television has played a prominent role in my life and the entire world. We could only get channel 4 from Bloomington and channel 6 from Indy. We watched Captain Video, cartoons, Uncle Miltie, Eddie Fisher, Arthur Godfrey, Perry Como, The Big Picture, the Friday Night Fights, Victory at Sea, Howdy Doody, and IU basketball sponsored by Chesty Potato Chips. The world came into our house every day with the news. The walls that isolated rural life from the world and held us captive were finally broken down like the Berlin Wall. But television has changed dramatically since that time of innocence.

Today TV is all about vulgarity and profanity, writhing and nearly naked people, destruction of property, violence, murder and mayhem, shouting, explosions, adultery and fornication, flaunting authority and breaking the rules. How times have changed.

I did not write the following ode or poem. I do not know who did. If I did that person would receive credit. However, the ode did strike a sympathetic chord on the harp that is my heart.

You could hardly see for all the snow,
Spread the rabbit ears as far as they go.
Pull a chair up to the TV set,
"Good night, David; Good night, Chet."

Depending on the channel you tuned,
You got Rob and Laura or Ward and June.
It felt so good, felt so right,
Life looked better in black and white.

I Love Lucy, The Real McCoys,
Dennis the Menace, the Cleaver boys,
"Rawhide", "Gunsmoke", "Wagon Train",
"Superman", Jimmy and Lois Lane.

"Father Knows Best", Patty Duke,
"Rin Tin Tin" and "Lassie" too,
Donna Reed on Thursday night,
Life looked better in black and white.

I wanna go back to black and white,
Everything always turned out right.
Simple people, simple lives,
Good guys always won the fights.

Now nothing is the way it seems,
In living color on the TV screen.
Too many murders, too much fight,
I wanna go back to black and white.

In God they trusted, in bed they slept,
A promise made was a promise kept.
They never cussed or broke their vows,
They'd never make the network now.

But if I could, I'd rather be,
In a TV town in '53,
It felt so good, felt so right,
Life looked better in black and white.

I'd trade all the channels on the satellite,
If I could just turn back the clock tonight.
To when everybody knew wrong from right,
Life was better in black and white.

Yes, We Watched the Radio

It seems so strange but when I was growing up in the country north of Calvertville in Highland Township, I remember listening to and watching the radio as a family. Geezers can remember radio, television without a picture. Yes, we sat and watched the radio as we ate apples and popcorn. I visualized how everyone looked and that caused me to visualize scenes and activities through their words. Today young people would say, "How weird! You watched the radio! I never look at the radio it is just on and makes sounds so I listen. How bizarre is that?"

To put this story in perspective, we lived in the country. We did not have electricity until long after W.W. II ended. To you that are still learning, America was involved in military action in World War II from December 1941 until September 1945. We had a battery powered upright Philco radio made by the Ford Company. It stood about three and a half feet high and was about two feet wide and about a foot deep. Batteries were not cheap to depression-laden folks. Some people would bring the car battery into the house and hook the radio to it. The car battery would be recharged in the normal operation of the vehicle.

In the early 1960's a friend gave me a Zenith upright radio circa 1930's. It was 42 inches high, 28 inches wide and 15 inches deep. It was in the bedroom where I slept while staying with he and his wife for a few days. I played it each day because it produced such dulcet tones. Later my daughter refinished it for a 4-H project and won a blue ribbon. She still has it in her home and it is a jewel.

The radio is a Zenith Automatic Short Wave Radio. The dial has Switzerland, South America, Japan, England, Morocco, Australia, Spain, France, Germany, Italy, Holland and the USA as countries one could listen to. The lower half of the dial lists as general broadcast, ships at sea, amateur, phone code and aviation police. I don't know what all of those mean.

The dial is round with curved glass and the tuner/dial is shaped like a lightning bolt or Z. On either side of the dial are six buttons. The left buttons read voice, normal, treble, alto, bass and low bass. The right buttons listed radio stations that could be tuned in similar to push button radios in cars today. The legible stations listed are WLW, WGN and WIRE.

There is an ensemble of tubes in the back that looks like a city skyline. There is also a large cardboard box that houses the antenna. A label reads Zenith Rotor Wavemagnet and it has a big horseshoe magnet pictured. There is a 15-inch speaker hiding behind the cloth cover in the front. When it speaks, people listen. It is glorious. TW says it is in retirement now but just a short time ago it played quite well.

In my kidhood the family would gather in the living room in the evening and turn on the radio. Out of the speaker would come the thrilling sounds of the "William Tell Overture" and then the announcer would say, "Return with us now to the thrilling days of yesteryear. From out of the past comes the thundering hoof beats of the great horse Silver. It is time for the Lone Ranger." I could see the silver colored horse, the brave masked man known as the Lone Ranger, his stalwart Indian companion

Tonto and later his nephew Dan Matthews. They rode the West and maintained law and order. I saw it all.

On another evening we heard, "Who knows what evil lurks in the hearts and minds of men, The Shadow Knows." This was followed by an ominous, creepy and sinister laugh. It was a program about a detective who fought evildoers. I did not know for a long time that the word shadow meant someone who followed or tailed people such as a private detective or private eye. I thought the program was about a real shadow. I was just a kid! "The Green Hornet" was a similar crime fighting show along with "Gangbusters." We captured many crooks.

I remember Jack Benny, saying, "Jello everybody, welcome to the show." The Jello Company sponsored him. We laughed about how stingy he was. I remember Mary his wife, Don Wilson his pal, Rochester the butler, Dennis the goofy one and the old Maxwell car. How we roared with laughter about the hilarious incidents he got into.

Then there were Fred Allen, Red Skelton, Fibber McGee and Molly and the hilarious antics of Amos and Andy, a couple of guys from Pine Ridge, Arkansas. During the day mom watched "Helen Trent" and "My Gal Sunday." I can still hear the organ music. She also watched the "50 - 50 Club" with Ruth Lyons. Later most teens listened to Easy Guinn on WIBC Indy in the afternoon as he played requests for dewy-eyed adolescents. I sent a request one time and remember being a bit embarrassed upon hearing it.

Those were the days my friend, I thought they'd never end. A time when I was more innocent, the world seemed safer and humor was more tasteful.

Outside vs. Inside

I live in Geezerville and therefore I have battles with inner perceptions and outward realities. It is truly amazing the great difference between what I believe and feel and what is. Now don't get me started on the meaning of "is", President Clinton. But I do struggle with the discrepancy of the two.

- On the inside my face is as smooth as a baby's hinder, but on the outside the wrinkles on my face are so deep they hold an inch of rain.

- On the inside my hair is still blonde, curly and luxurious, but on the outside I look like an old Larry of the Three Stooges.

- On the inside my hands could be used for television jewelry commercials, but on the outside liver spots make my hands look like I have been painting the Brooklyn Bridge with a toothbrush.

- On the inside my abdomen is ripped and I have a six-pack working, but on the outside my equator bulges more than the earth's equator.

- On the inside I see the face of a young man, just out of college starting a family and career, but on the outside my face looks like it has worn out three bodies

- On the inside I feel like I could have won the pole vault in the 2004 Olympics, but on the outside I can't even jump to conclusions.

- On the inside my teeth still flash in the sun like Carly Patterson, Olympic skater and All American girl, but on the outside my teeth sparkle like a swamp buggy that just completed the bog race at the Muddy Gras Red Neck Olympics.

- On the inside I could win the slam-dunk contest at the high school All Star Game, but on the outside I can't even slam the car door.

- On the inside I can cover more center field than Mickey Mantle and Curt Flood combined, but on the outside I can't even cover a refrigerator bowl with Saran Wrap or Glad Press 'n Seal.
- On the inside I could shoot a gnat off a moose's nose at two miles with a Kentucky long rifle, but on the outside I wear glasses to find my glasses.
- On the inside I am still wearing a spiffy flat top so stiff with butch hair wax that it could pierce a No. 10 washtub, but on the outside I have so much hair in my ears and nose and my bushy eyebrows make me look like a bald werewolf.
- On the inside my fingers still look like they did when I was taking typing in high school, but on the outside my fingernails have more ridges than the Appalachian Mountains.
- On the inside I am still convinced that I have a better looking nose than Paul Newman, but on the outside my nose continues to grow like the national debt.
- On the inside I have a better looking neck than Arnold Schwartzenegger, but on the outside my neck looks like I have swallowed a rhinoceros and it is still lodged in my throat.

- On the inside the back of my neck is as smooth as Dick Lugar running for reelection, but on the outside I have more wrinkles than a clown suit after a six-month run of Ringling Brothers and Barnum & Bailey circus.

- On the inside I could win "Jeopardy", "Who Wants to Be a Millionaire" and "Two for the Money" every day, but on the outside my brain is slower than the traffic in Branson, Missouri.

- On the inside my joints are quieter than Rush Limbaugh at a senate hearing on illegal drug use, but on the outside my joints make more noise than a thrashing machine.

- On the inside I feel like I could whip my weight in wildcats, but on the outside I have trouble whipping Jello and Cool-Whip.

A Geezer's idea of getting lucky,—Found his car in the parking lot.

When I Smell New Mown Hay I think about Dad

When I smell gas and oil I think about working in a service station back in the 1950s and early sixties. I remember BW's dad working for Wilson Short in the Shell Station and then for Doc Pickard in the Cities Service. Then he bought the Cities Service and operated it for many years even after it became Citgo.

When I smell fried chicken I think about Mom and Sunday Dinner. She would whip up some wonderful meals for the five of us. People used to visit on Sunday afternoons. I remember sitting around visiting on summer days and winter evenings. I think about the family reunion at the Bloomfield Park when all of the aunts and uncles and cousins would pile into the park, eat until they almost burst and then spend the afternoon getting reacquainted. What memories. I think of Nora Caton who fried chicken in real lard. It was so unhealthy but Col. Sanders never served chicken so good. It was larapin'. Down South larapin' means better than good.

When I smell freshly mowed grass I think about the old reel mower that we had on the farm. It would not cut melted butter. The crabgrass would make it ride up and skip along on top of the grass. The reel would stop and the wheels would skid and it was impossible to mow. I remember Uncle Frank and Aunt Flossie Wilson had a new gas powered mower that we borrowed on occasion. It was wonderful. I miss them.

When I smell a freshly cut watermelon I think of Grandpa Price. On hot summer days when the white clouds plowed across the sky like sheep tumbling out of the barn or marshmallows pouring out of the sack, he took Brother and me across the mighty White River on a safari to steal watermelons. We did that several times and we felt like Caribbean Pirates or Vikings. Later he 'fessed up that he knew the farmer who said he could have all he wanted. Burst our bubble. I think of 4-H meetings in the summer under the tutelage of L.C. McIntosh long time teacher and FFA and 4-H Leader. I wish I could go back and attend some of the meetings and eat watermelon. Some of those members are now great grandparents. Those thoughts are tucked away in my memory bank and they come pouring out from time to time.

When I smell mint or spearmint I am driving my 1938 Ford out on the town with my sweet face by my side. Back then there were no bucket seats so your main squeeze could sit next to you. There were bucket seats but they were at the feed mill, the Calvertville store or in the milking stall where the bucket was turned upside down and used as a seat. I always chewed Wrigley's Spearmint gum so my breath would be fresh in the clinches, if you know what I mean. Drive-in movies, regular movies, fairs, ball games and Sunday afternoon dates were all Wrigley Times.

When I smell fresh baked bread I think of home. Mom's kitchen was always redolent with the delightful aroma of yeast rolls, Clabber Girl powder biscuits or pies. If I close my eyes I can see hot homemade butter melting on a roll then slathered with homemade blackberry jelly, washed down with cold milk. Pies baked in a 12-inch glass dish. Sawmill gravy running down the side of the biscuits with bacon or ham in the morning. No five-star restaurant in the land ever made any better. Thanks Mom, for everything.

When I smell new mown hay with all its fragrance I think of my life with Dad on the farm. When we put up hay it was always stifling hot and humid. Sweat would pour off of us like Secretary Rumsfeld trying to explain where the weapons of mass destruction went. It was hot in the field when we loaded the hay and even hotter in the loft where we had to mow it back for storage. I recall a time when we were sweating a load of hay into the barn and we heard the rain crow. In essence it was a dove. As boys we thought that when the rain crow sang it meant that rain was imminent. I didn't know the word imminent then. We just thought it was going to rain soon. We beseeched the crow to bring it on so we could go to the house. It didn't and we didn't until the work was done. Later the three of us played the hay field world series in that field. I miss my Dad so much. I owe him everything.

Smells can take us on trips to the past and cause us to remember the delightful moments of our lives.

Life Was Good, It Still Is

When I smell popcorn I think of home. Back in my salad days when the family wanted to go on a trip to the "Snackmosphere" I had a job to do. I don't know how we made it but we did not have a microwave oven that has a button to push for popcorn. We did not go to the store and purchase popcorn in the antiseptic hermetically sealed bags. We grew the popcorn, husked it and then shelled it from the cob. The next step was to stir and blow. The stirring brought small particles of lint like pieces to the top. Blowing removed it from the kernels before popping. It was much like winnowing grain in the old, old days. I am not that old.

My official title was Sir Popper of Corn. I was the Orville Redenbacher of the household;

"Sir Snacksalot." Mom had an aluminum pan with a lid that was the official popper. I would introduce an appropriate quantity of lard into it, then add a copious measure of salt and heat. In the fullness of time, not a nanosecond too soon the corn was added like rain from the sky. When the first kernel popped the lid was added and then the shake and heat process began. Heat, pop, shake, heat, pop, shake. When the popping ceased the ambrosia of the cornfield was then distributed into bowls and served with another generous blizzard of salt. Most of the time we had apples to eat with the corn. Glory it was good. I can taste it now.

When I smell popcorn I think of The State Theater and the many hours I spent there with my sweet face. You think popcorn is good. I held my "Sir Snacksalot" role in abeyance and became "Sir Nuddle", if you know what I mean.

Now when I smell popcorn I think about high school gymnasiums and basketball. It is the first thing you smell when you enter a gym. When you see a high school principal at a basketball game or football game he or she is not there to enjoy the game or to socialize. He or she would likely rather be somewhere else. He or she is on patrol like Barney Fife looking for trouble and trying to prevent it. Monday morning I had to clean up the mess left over from the Friday and Saturday night games: fights, name calling, band problems, parental complaints about officiating or the coaches or players. I couldn't eat popcorn for many years after my stint as a principal.

When I smell salt air and the ocean I think about my hitch in the U.S. Navy. I wish I could say that I was involved in one of the great battles of American History as we fought valiantly against a masterful foe in the stormy, icy north Atlantic keeping America safe. Alas I served between wars on a minesweeper, a wooden bucket called the Swerve MSO495 out of Charleston, South Carolina. The only things I battled were seasickness, practice mines and Navy regulations.

I clearly remember the first few times we put out to sea and I talked to Old Roark several times. When you stand at the railing and all of the muscles in your body lock and you share your breakfast, lunch, dinner from the past three days, with the fish, it is called talking to Old Roark. Think of the sounds one makes when throwing up, out and down. I remember being in storms at sea when the bow of the ship would plunge under the water and wondering if it was going to come up again. I remember sailors going on liberty and coming back in bad shape.

When I smell summer evenings I think about home. In the summer as the sun goes down and a faint cool breeze blows in from the West with a sprinkling of corn tassel aroma on it like powdered sugar on a pound cake, I think of home. When that breeze is flavored with a bit of new mown hay, and the dampness of the night air that is cool to the touch, I am a kid again. I'm back with Mom and Dad, my sister "the killer" and my big brother on the farm. Just about dark thirty we would be resting on the porch or in the yard just about to pop after eating one of Mom's great feasts. Lightning bugs would flit around the yard and garden then out to the hayfield and pasture. Animals were settling down for the night to the song of the hoot owl and the whippoorwill. The perfume of peonies, iris and roses permeated the cool air. Mom's old- fashioned rose bush in the corner of the yard would be outdoing itself. I was Content. Life was good. It still is.

Halloween Isn't What It Used to Be

I remember Halloween of my youth and the generation before me, being times of more tricks than treats. Men would sit around the stove in the Calvertville Store, Dixon's Barber Shop or the Knights of Pythias Lodge Hall, gasconading (lying or exaggerating and boasting) about the tricks they had committed on All Hallows Eve in years gone by.

They roared with laughter and told stories about turning over outhouses and disassembling wagons and then reassembling them on the roof of a barn. I do not understand how that was done. Wagons are quite heavy barn roofs are quite high and who had the strength to do such things. I wonder. They also told of removing wheels from cars or jacking them up and putting blocks under the frame so it could not move. Another trick I heard people talk about was tacking. The perpetrators would stick a nail up under the siding of a house. A string would be tied to the nail and a horseshoe or another metal object would be suspended on the string. Then another long string would be attached to the shoe and strung out through the yard a safe distance from the house. The perpetrators would then yank on the string causing the object to bang against the house thus annoying sleepers. I heard stories about some men who would sneak out of the house, find the string and then shoot a shotgun along the string toward the malefactors. Truth? I do not know. Many times the truth would not be allowed to get in the way of a good story.

In my trick or treating days we would throw shelled corn, soap windows and I admit I helped turn over **one** outhouse in Worthington. The owner chased us. We got away. My outhouse tipping ended and my life of crime except that one time.

It was one of those blustery nights in late October approaching Halloween. The air was redolent with the smell of burning leaves. The full moon was ducking in and out of the clouds as they skittered across the sky like children playing tag on the school ground.   I was hitchhiking home to Calvertville from basketball practice at Worthington High School as many did. That is until we became old enough and could afford to drive. I knew everyone I rode with. On this particular evening, two older high school guys, who shall remain nameless, gave me a ride. About a mile out of town, highway 157 crossed the White River on a single lane, very old iron bridge. The East half of the bridge flooring was concrete but the west half was wooden creosoted planking. Creosote is a petroleum derivative and is flammable.

Did I say it was close to Halloween?   We approached the bridge, from the West and all was going well. Suddenly at mid-point, the driver stopped the car. The two guys bailed out of the car, ripped a bale of straw from the trunk, yanked the wires off and spread the straw into a loose pile on the bridge flooring. Well, I was born at night but it wasn't last night. I could see what they were going to do. They waited until they saw the headlights of an approaching car. When the car came close, these two scofflaws set the straw on fire, leaped into the car, sped off the bridge and careened down a small road next to the river. From that vantagepoint we watched the scene unfold.

The car slowed, moved closer and stopped, at a safe distance and then turned around and went back to Worthington.

My two traveling companions were laughing deliriously. This was a spectacular Halloween stunt for them and they were reveling in it. Not I. I was petrified because I feared that the bridge floor would catch on fire and then the people who depended upon that bridge would have to travel more than thirty miles or more through Bloomfield to get to their destination. My short life passed before my eyes. I visualized myself sitting in a jail cell playing a harmonica and singing, "Nobody Knows the Trouble I've Seen." I slunk down in the back seat to hide. I was miserable.

The flaming straw was like the burning of Atlanta or Dresden. As I watched, it seemed to roar and billow out over the top of the superstructure of the bridge hundreds of feet in the air. Well, it seemed like it. I thought, "I am a dead man and I'm not even a man yet." Fortunately the straw burned rather quickly and the blustery wind blew much of it off the side and into the river below where it hissed, seethed and then quickly extinguished. Soon we were on our way home again. No harm done. This time. Halloween isn't what it used to be.

Winter in Yesteryear Redux

In a previous story I discussed wintertime in the good old days. This story continues where that one ended.

Winter was a slow time for most farmers. Life moved almost as fast as a glacier. Mother Nature and the pace of living slowed down while everything hunkered down and waited for spring. Snow piled onto the corn stalks and into the fence rows. Mice, owls, hawks, raccoons, opossums, foxes, squirrels and other critters would forage through every inch of soil looking for food to survive.

Farmers would go to town or to the store to run some errands or to just loaf. Many a time I have been in Gar Wells' blacksmith shop in

Worthington and listened to the crowd socializing and gasconading – stretching the truth, lying and having a good time. The uniform of the day consisted of long sleeved blue chambray shirts, sweatshirts, bib overalls with galluses, old sweaters, boots, and heavy caps with earflaps on them. Some wore pants with wide, heavy braces – suspenders. There was no coat rack so coats would be hung on a peg or laid across tools waiting for pickup. The forge provided the needed warmth for the shop. Men would sit on boxes, nail kegs, old wooden chairs and blocks of wood and talk, tell stories, kid each other in a relaxed, warm environment of esprit de corps. This scene was repeated in the Calvertville store, the feed mill and the barbershop. What I would give to join in such a conversation today.

My brother, sister and I would race the Grim Reaper and certain death by freezing as we charged down the frozen lane from the house to the school bus. The wind would roar around me trying to get inside my clothing to get warm. I was convinced that there was nothing between the North Pole and me but a barbed wire fence and it had blown down.

Mom still had to do the washing in the coldest weather. I couldn't figure it out but clothes would freeze dry. When I helped Mom with the laundry I remember how my wet hands would sting moving between the hot clothes and the cold winds that blew while I hung up the clothing. I was glad to get back in the house. Later when I brought them in they were as stiff as Al Gore dancing at the Democratic Convention.

The outhouse was a place called Ft. Necessity. One did not stay very long to read the paper or the catalog. It was in and out and back to the house. Sometimes it was so frosty that there was no contact between the seat and my seat if you know what I mean.

When I was quite young we would take the horses to the Calvertville feed mill on Saturday. They would move very slowly through the dug road because of the ice. The dug road was about a quarter mile from our house and cut through the side of the hill under a canopy of trees. Horse pulled slip scrapers and shovels dug it as part of a WPA project and it has always been the dug road to me. Often Dad would lead them to give them confidence and to guide them in the least slick way. I don't know how they pulled the wagon full of corn and three guys over the huge hill. Going up was difficult but going down seemed more egregious.

Brother and I played ice hockey on the frozen ponds. We used a can as a puck and bent sticks for the hockey sticks. Sometimes we used brooms. I won many a Stanley Cup in my day. I would humiliate him almost every time we played. When not playing hockey we roared down the hill on our sleds and sheet iron roofing. We would go down the hill like a rocket sled. What fun we had.

Our animals did not spend much time outside on really cold, gray, gloomy days. They would venture out to get a drink at the trough and then go back inside. We did too.

School was in session every day. It was never called off or delayed. We went every day. Unlike my ancestors who walked ten miles to school in the snow up hill both ways, we only walked down the lane to the bus. There were many times when we almost did not get over the hill but Mac persevered and we made it.

People were tougher back then. It is true. Most people today are not outside much at all. They run from the house to the car that takes five seconds and then drive to work or school. They take 10 seconds to run inside and reverse the process in the evening. They drive to the store or theater and run inside taking 10 to 20 seconds and complain how cold it is. In my kidhood we spent many hours outside. We played and also worked cleaning out the barn, cutting wood and bringing in coal, shoveling snow and feeding animals. We also milked cows every day. People were tougher. Old timers complain, "We never called off school back in the good old days. Now it seems like three snow flakes per acre and school is off for two days." It is true. Student safety is the major thrust of school closing decisions. Students are not as strong as they once were and not accustomed to being exposed to extreme temperatures. Like it or lump it that is true. They also travel much farther than in the past.

The past is a wonderful place to visit but most of us do not want to live there again. The best part about the past is that I was younger and was going to grab the world by the tail and hold on. Someone must have greased that tail because I never could get a firm grip on it. It got away from me.

Dan Gill

ICE
CREAM

If you have ever had your lip
stuck to an ice cream dipper,
you may be a geezer.

An Old Dude Beat Me!

"Summer time and the livin' is easy, fish are jumpin' and the cotton is high." [Hint: It is a song.] It is from the excellent folk opera Porgy and Bess by George Gershwin set in Charleston, South Carolina. Livin' is a little easier in the summertime which brings me to this story.

I live with the president. How about that? BW is a member of two home extension clubs and served as county president last year and signed on again for next year. Recently one of her clubs decided to hold their regular meeting at the park and invite husbands. In honor of Clayton Bulwer Lytton, "It was a hot and humid day." Bob and I were relegated to cooking burgers and dogs on one of those park grills that always look like someone had just broiled a pterodactyl on it without removing the entrails or the feathers. Do pterodactyls have feathers? Look it up. Thank you Mr. Kaiser for inventing tin foil and phasing out your car. If you remember the Kaiser and Frasier cars you have some age spots in places you don't want to reveal.

BW, always the optimist, thinks that people are going to play games at every event she attends so she packed the croquet set and a plastic set of horseshoes which are as close to useless and pitiful as one can get. As Bob and I cooked, Samantha (Sam), his ten year-old granddaughter showed some interest in the horseshoe game. Sam is a city girl and for reasons too broad for this story she has missed out on skill development that I find necessary for a good life. I took a break from my culinary responsibilities to join her. She knew very little about the game so I tutored her.

Then I set up the croquet game. Bob cooked the burgers until they could do no harm to anyone. The dogs looked like huge pencil leads when they finished their trial by fire. The ladies brought food so lunch was shall we say a typical BBQ with all of the trimmings. It was larapin' as they say in Kentucky. Absolutely beyond good over in the finger lickin' good category. The delicious needle was pegged on "P" for phantasmagorical.

Sam couldn't skip rocks either. My dad taught my brother and me how to skip rocks at an early age. Sam and I sauntered over to the creek that runs through the park and found a very large area of smooth, flat creek rocks many ideal for skipping. She picked up a stone and tried to throw it backhanded like a Frisbee. She hit a boy, about her age, on the leg with such a force that it would have killed a Grand Daddy Long Legs, maybe. She apologized profusely and the boy feigned serious harm. No harm no foul. I tutored, "Select a good rock, bend your knees, lean over a bit and throw the rock in a forward sidearm motion." Her first two plunked but the third skipped three times. She was exultant. "I have never been able to skip a rock before," she gushed. Then it was Katie bar the door. She was on fire.

The coup de grace, however, was basketball. She borrowed a ball and asked me to play. Remember I have passed 13 lustrums in age. I played basketball in high school and in the Navy but since then only in pickup games and none in this century and few in the last quarter of the past century.

Did I say it was hot and humid? Sam is a neophyte and has limited experience but what she lacked in ability she made up for in energy. She bounced, jumped and moved like one of those rubber balls attached to a paddle with a long rubber band. She was moving like a beekeeper with a hole in his bonnet; like a tornado through a trailer park. She was everywhere but in "Effectiveville."

I moved with the grace of Babe The Blue Ox wearing lead boots with no oxygen bottle near the summit of Mt. Everest. Tsunami sized drops of sweat poured off my follicular challenged head. I tried to lose. She dribbled then double dribbled then flung the ball at the goal. I wouldn't quite call it a shot! Her greatest thrill must result from hitting a three-point shot which she tried frequently [with no success]. I showed her how to hold the ball and how to use her legs and wrist in shooting.

Alas and alack! I beat her four straight games of horse and pig by hitting layups and I bungled many of them on purpose. She could not hit the red side of a green barn painted purple. Then she asked, "Why don't we play a regular game?" "Okay." So we played and miraculously I won while trying to lose. Late in the game she said, to no one in particular, "I can't believe it! An old dude is beating me at my best game." That sorta spoiled the thrill of victory, I thought, suppressing a giggle.

Humorous anecdotes about Grandkids

BW and I went to breakfast at a restaurant where the "Senior's Special" was two eggs, bacon, hash browns and toast for $1.99.

"Sounds good," BW said, "But I don't want the eggs."

Susie Server warned, "Then I have to charge you two dollars and forty-nine cents because you're ordering a la carte."

"You mean I'd have to pay for not taking the eggs?" BW said incredulously, "then I'll take the special."

"How do you want your eggs?"

"Raw and in the shell," BW replied. She took the two eggs home. Don't mess with Geezers.

*****

A grandson was visiting his grandmother one day when he asked, "Grandma, do you know how you and God are alike?" Grandma polished her halo and responded, "No, how are we alike?"

"You're both old," he said.

*****

Granddad and his little grandson, Jeff, whose face was sprinkled with bright freckles, spent the day at the zoo. Many children were waiting in line to get their cheeks painted by a local artist who was decorating them with tiger paws.

A girl in line next to Jeff said, "You've got too many freckles, there's no place to paint!" This embarrassed Jeff and he dropped his head. Grandpa knelt down beside him and said, "I love your freckles. When I was a little boy I always wanted freckles,' he said while tracing his finger across the little boy's cheek. "Freckles are beautiful!"

Jeff looked up, "Really?" "Of course," said Grandpa, "Why just name me one thing that's prettier than freckles."

Jeff thought for a moment, peered intensely into his Grandpa's face and softly whispered, "Wrinkles."

*****

Students study about public servants in the early grades of school. When Jeff was in the third grade his teacher asked him to write a sentence about a public servant. He wrote, "The fireman came down the ladder pregnant." Mrs. Wilson took the lad aside to correct him. "Don't you know what pregnant means?" she asked. "Sure," Jeff said confidently. "It means carrying a child."

*****

Seven-year old Jessica surprised her grandmother one morning by making her coffee. Grandmother drank what was the worst cup of coffee in her life. When she got to the bottom, there were three of those little green plastic army men in the cup. She asked, "Jessica, why are these army men in my coffee?"

Jessica replied, "Grandma, it says on TV, The best part of waking up is soldiers in your cup."

*****

Grandmothers are moms with lots of frosting

Grandmothers are just antique little girls.

Perfect love sometimes does not come until the first grandchild. Welsh proverb

When grandparents enter the door, discipline flies out the window. Ogden Nash

Grandma always makes you feel she has been waiting to see just you all day and now the day is complete. Marcy DeMaree

Grandmas never run out of hugs or cookies.

Grandparents hold our tiny hands for just a little while, but our hearts forever.

Grandchildren are God's way of compensating us for growing old. Mary H. Waldrip

Grandparent grandchild relationships are simple. Grandparents are short on criticism and long on love.

A grandparent is old on the outside but young on the inside.

One of the most powerful handclasps is that of a new grandbaby around the finger of a grandfather.

Grandparents pretend that they don't know you on Halloween.

A Blast From the Past

How many of these words and phrases do you remember? Did you use them? Were they important to your everyday communications with significant others?

Fender skirts – What a great blast from the past! I haven't thought about fender skirts in years. When I was a teenager, I considered it such a funny term but you had to have them to be in style. They made me think of a car in a dress. Thinking about fender skirts started me thinking about other words that quietly disappear from our language with hardly a notice. Duals? Exhaust pipes.

I saw a car with Curb feelers on it recently. It was an old car that had been restored. Curb feelers and steering knobs are out of the vocabulary of today. Some elderly person over 40 will have to be brought in to discuss and explain those terms to this generation. I remember them well.

Remember continental kits? They were rear bumper extenders and spare tire covers that were supposed to make any car as cool as a Lincoln Continental. It never worked, in my estimation. They were very effective in causing scabs on shins and busted many a kneecap but mostly they looked stupid. You don't put a Rolex in a Timex case.

When did we quit calling them emergency brakes? At some point parking brake became the popular term. But I miss the hint of drama that went with emergency brake.

I'm sad too, that almost all the old folks are gone who would call the accelerator the foot feed. And we never use the choke any more since vehicles don't have them or carburetors either for that matter. How about the throttle that was the prehistoric cruise control?

I used to hear this phrase quite often when I was in my salad days and I still use it but no one younger than I include it in his vocabulary. The phrase is store bought. Of course just about everything is store bought these days. But once it was bragging material to have a store-bought dress or shirt or a store bought bag of candy. And a store bought hair cut was special too.

Coast to coast is a phrase that once held all sorts of excitement and now means almost nothing. Now we take the term worldwide for granted. We even talk glibly about outer space and interstellar space missions are becoming more common.

I remember when people used to discuss wall-to-wall carpeting in the home. It was magical and if a house had wall-to-wall carpeting that was special. Those folks were wealthy. Back in the middle of the last century when I was a boy, people [well some didn't] covered their hardwood floors with wall-to-wall carpeting. Today, everyone [there is one person in Iowa who doesn't] replaces their wall-to-wall carpeting with hardwood floors. How about that!

When was the last time you heard the quaint phrase 'in a family way?' It's hard to imagine that the word pregnant was once considered a little too graphic, a little too clinical for use in polite company. So people had to talk about the stork visits and being in a family way or simply expecting. Today when someone reports that Amy is expecting I always ask, "Expecting what?" That is always followed by a well deserved slap to my face. No one likes a smart aleck. There is a term I don't hear either. Today couples say, "We are expecting." I have lived a long time and I have never known a man to be pregnant. But I am out of the loop.

Apparently brassiere is a word no longer in usage. I said it the other day and my wife and daughter cackled. I guess it is just bra now. Unmentionables probably wouldn't be understood at all. I suppose that skivvies would be gauche also.

It is hard to recall that this word was once said in a whisper – divorce. And no one is called a divorcee anymore, certainly not a gay divorcee. Come to think of it, confirmed bachelors and career girls are long gone too.

Another phrase that I don't hear any more is "going to town to do the tradin'" which meant to go shopping. I never saw people trade for items but they still used the phrase.

Geezer of long ago, especially those who lived in the country would use the word mess when referring to food. They would say, "There is just enough green beans in the garden for a mess" or "we had a mess of mushrooms yesterday." Of course mess is a military term still in use today.

Most of these words go back to the 1950s and before, but here is a pure 1960s phrase I came across the other day – rat fink. Ooh what a nasty put-down.

Here is a word I miss – percolator. That was just a fun word to say. And what was it replaced with? Coffeemaker. How dull. They are made in "Dullaware." Mr. Coffee, I blame you for this.

I miss those made-up marketing words that were meant to sound so modern and now sound so retro and jaded. Words like dynaflow and electraluxe. Introducing the 1963 Admiral TV now with SpectraVision.

Was there a telethon that wiped out lumbago? Nobody complains of that anymore. Dropsy. Maybe that is what castor oil cured, because I never hear mothers threatening their kids with castor oil anymore either. Spring tonic. Epizootic. Asafetida bag.

Some words aren't gone, but are definitely on the endangered list. The one that grieves me the most is supper.

BW Had a Terrible, Horrible, Who Would Have Thought It Possible Kind of Day

Have you ever had a day that made you wish that you had stayed in bed? BW did recently. The first part of the day was uneventful. That is until she went to the bank. She parked beside the front door, as all Americans want to do, went inside completed her banking then returned to the car but could not start it. No keys! She ripped every pocket wrong side out, used a Geiger counter to check every inch of the area between the car and inside the bank, pillaged through every pocket and opening in her purse – that took about three hours; well you know about women and their purses. Finally, she took the last resort and called me, "Captain Recovery to the Rescue", who brought an extra key to the scene. She still has not found her keys.

She, like everyone else, spent the remainder of the day tracing and retracing her steps at the bank trying to remember where the keys could be. Like your tongue that keeps feeling the tooth with the lost filling, she kept going back to the problem. She prowled around the house like a lion in a cage, pawing, snorting and growling. She called the bank and had people look. No luck. She ripped her car apart like a greaser in a chop shop using an acetylene torch before shipping the pieces to Mexico. Nothing. Late in the day the phone rang and it was one of her friends in the County Home Extension Group – BW is the president. The friend called to determine if BW was ill or had been in an accident. She said, "We were just wondering why you missed the sewing class today." Aargh! She forgot all about it.

The ultimate frustration, the topper, the coup de grace, occurred later in the evening of the same day. BW was feeling downhearted and a bit depressed so she decided to provide solace for her feelings with a huge bowl of Yogen Fruz. That is what Canadians call frozen yogurt in Ontario Province. We have made concessions to age and health and for years we have been eating frozen yogurt instead of ice cream. I have almost forgotten what real ice cream tastes like so I am able to convince myself that yogurt tastes good. I have done the same with turkey bacon, egg substitutes, turkey ham and bologna instead of the real stuff, spread instead of butter and one percent milk instead of regular sweet milk as my mother called it.

BW extricated the 55 gallon barrel of yogurt from the freezer, dipped a prodigious quantity into a bowl that when full would have served a large family of Katrina victims for several days. Before she drizzled some Three Musketeer Chocolate sauce and sprinkled on a copious quantity of crushed almonds on the yogurt, she was faced with a dilemma. What to do with the ice cream dipper? She had purchased a new metal dipper that resembled the old fashioned ones used in ice cream parlors and general stores in the vaunted days of yesteryear. And therein lies a new story.

There was yogurt residue on the dipper so being the lover of yogurt that she is, she could not resist placing it in her mouth to lick it like an ice cream cone, forgetting for the moment that it was metal. Yoikes! Much to her chagrin the scoop stuck to the inside of her upper lip. Have you ever seen a grown woman with an ice cream scoop protruding from her face, shrieking like a Rock and Roll Guitar player who has just received a 10,000 volt shock from his electric guitar? I hadn't either until then. Now we have all heard of the little boy who on a day in February when it was colder than a mother-in-law's kiss got his tongue stuck on the school flagpole. We have laughed at such sport. We have also heard of some men and high school aged "doofases" who have done similar dumb things on a bet or after consuming too much of a distilled beverage. But, I have never heard of a woman getting her lip stuck on an ice cream dipper in the kitchen. She wailed like a pig caught in the fence as she pulled it away ripping away enough skin to make two footballs. Her growls would scare a lion out of tall grass. Several drivers on highway 267 that is about four blocks away from our house drove to the side because they thought they heard an approaching emergency vehicle. I haven't laughed that hard since I witnessed the impertinent gall of Teddy Kennedy questioning the character and values of a Supreme Court nominee.

For the next two or three days BW's lip looked like she had gone six rounds with Muhammed Ali and lost. The Pointless Pugilist of Plainfield. What a day!

Technology Is To Blame!

There are more Americans alive today than at any other time in history yet more and more people report that they are lonely and lack meaningful human companionship. Relationships are in rack and ruin. I wonder why?

Could it be that the fast-paced, high-tech American existence has taken a toll on the civility and graciousness of our society? From the road rage in the morning commute to the high decibel of cell-phone conversations that ruin dinner out, men and women behaving badly and feeling isolated have become the hallmark of a hurry-up, fast food attitude and me first life style in America.

People are more self-absorbed than ever and in greater numbers. People fear to go out in some places afraid of being harmed. The media gorges itself on stories of murder, hijackings, drug gangs that plague city and county, gang violence and the awful rotten things that people do to one another. Too many Americans exhibit the highest need for instant gratification that strains common courtesies to the breaking point.

I believe another culprit that is ravaging the land and world is the tremendous explosion and advancement in the field of technology. Affluent young adults and teens especially have nothing but the conveniences of computers and cell phones, devices that take them away from face-to-face encounters and can be extremely annoying in a crowd or audience.

Technology is producing a society that is more and more isolated from actual contact with other people. It is only through actual contact with others that we observe civility, practice courtesy and learn to interact with others in a genteel and cordial way. Without such encounters people become grunting, flailing troglodytes who have no concern for the way others feel or how they are affected by "my" behavior.

Where is this cell phone pandemic going to end? People are concerned with flu epidemics and bird flu. I am concerned about cell flu. Phones now send pictures, download music, take pictures send messages and cut your hair. Some use earplugs that further isolate them from others. No eye contact is allowed.

Restaurants, coffee shops, airplanes, lounges and office buildings are using WiFi so one can further isolate oneself while eating, drinking or traveling. Today we can bank at home, pay at the pump, get a college degree and then an advanced degree, shop for groceries, purchase many other needed items and get our mail on line or by cell phone. We can down load movies, get our license plates renewed, do research and write online, publish a book, and work at home via the Internet. And never see or interact with another person. How awful.

Police agencies have stationed cameras at intersections that take pictures and send a ticket when you run a red light. I am waiting for the Cell Phone church where you can dial it in and fast forward through the boring parts, skip the contribution and the sermon and not spend more than three minutes at worship and never see or hear anyone yet have the feeling that I was there. Who is kidding whom?

I anticipate a future cell phone that can diagnose illness and send information down the line to the IU med center for information. Or you will be able to place the phone button side down on your chest. There will be built-in probes with small cameras and surgical instruments attached. At the proper signal, the phone will apply anesthesia and make the surgical entrance portals. Then the cameras and instruments will enter the body cavity and remove your appendix and gall bladder. It will then apply adhesive to the openings, seal them and you are on the way to your favorite coffee shop to share the experience online with someone in Australia. Anyone can do it if he spends at least one night at a Holiday Inn Express.

How I long for the days when people would sit on the front porch and visit with family and friends or they would sit around the potbellied stove in the country store eating crackers and cheese and sharing their lives with old friends. I remember Saturday nights in the country towns where I grew up. People would line the streets and park benches and talk to each other face-to-face. I remember the happy chatter and laughter around the Triangle in Worthington. How I long for the days when the old party line was the best communications device since the grapevine when people's lives were so intertwined with the community that relationships were more meaningful, life was less harried, people were more civil and polite and humor was less trenchant. Be well, laugh often and love much.

January sure is a long-g-g month.

A Cool, Soft Breeze Reminded Me of the Hot Days of Summer

Summer time is hot in Indiana. Don't doubt me on this as I have lived here for a long time. But you don't know hot until you have lived in the south in the summer. BW and I lived in Charleston, South Carolina for about three years while I was protecting the nation and its freedoms by serving in the Navy. It is hot and sticky. We also lived in Arkansas and Louisiana. The living was not easy. It was really bad during the dog days of summer. We never had air conditioning and we would sweat like Bill Clinton trying to define the word "is" or like Rush Limbaugh at a senate committee hearing on the illegal use of prescription drugs.

Sit up straight, pay attention because there will be a quiz later. Many ancient people observed the stars, played connect the dot, created constellations and gave them names. The ancient Romans gave us bears [Ursa major and Ursa minor] twins [Gemini] a bull [Taurus], dogs [Canis Major and Canis Minor], Hercules and many more. They gave the world the term "Dog days" to indicate the period of time that the constellation Canis Major [The Big Dog] was prominent in the summer sky. [You Purdue fans thought The Big Dog was Glen Robinson. Wrong again.] Sirius is the brightest star in Canis Major and at times it would seem to align with the sun. They blamed that alignment for causing the hot, sultry weather in late summer, hence they named the period the dog days of summer. Roughly it corresponds with August through mid-September. The real cause of the excessive heat is the tilt of the earth and its relationship with the sun. That is more than you wanted to know about that. End of lecture.

We live in a section of the nation that geographers refer to as humid continental. I don't want to insult your intelligence but that means in the summer time the living is not easy it is hot and sticky. We are now in the dog days of the summer. "On a hot, sticky day in late July or early August, the old timers down where I grew up used to say, "It sure is close today." The chickens in the barn lot would say, "It is a wing lifting day" as they lifted their wings up in an attempt to be cool. The pigs would say, "It is a mud wallowing day" as they flopped and rooted around in the muddy bog of the wallow.

Our two-story farmhouse had no air conditioning except in the winter. There was no insulation in it either when I was a whippersnapper. The house would be draped in heat and humidity as thick as a fog, a solid, pregnant, dense fog that none could penetrate. There was one window upstairs in the west room that served as a funnel to channel the heat and humidity from three counties into my room. There was also one in the East room. We three kids tried to sleep slathered in heat and humidity like sticky buns covered with icing. It would grip us like barnacles on the hull of a sinking ship. With our skin leaking like rusty tubs, we waited endlessly for a cool breeze to cool our hot sweaty bodies. Every small breeze was as welcome as soldiers returning in triumph from war. The slightest movement of air brought some relief. Late at night the room finally cooled and we drifted off to fitful slumber.

The windows had the weights inside the jam but they no longer worked. We used a stick to hold the window up or an expandable screen.

One Saturday night we went to town and some booboisie, okay I left the light on and forgot to put the screen in. When we came home there were about ten babillion bugs of every sort known to humanity in the room. Have you ever tried to sleep in a hot room with bugs crawling in your ears and eyes? Later we bought a fan that was as effective as Ross Perot's makeup man.

Americans are addicted to air conditioning and electricity. Recently the power had been off for several hours because of a storm. Our neighborhood was feeling the effects of the Dog Days. People looked like hush puppies bubbling in a pan of grease. Life came to a halt. Nothing works without electricity. Living is not easy. Fish weren't even jumpin' because they were too hot.

I walked out on the driveway and watched as the gloom of night covered the land as if some giant was pulling a thick, dark quilt over the earth. It was stifling. I thought of those steamy nights trying to sleep upstairs at home. Then I felt it; almost imperceptive; a cool, soft breeze blowing softly from the Southwest; a cooling, refreshing, barely perceptible, rejuvenating reprieve from heat and humidity. Just then power was restored. Cheers reverberated throughout the neighborhood.

A Coca Cola Bottle Became a Time Machine.

I stopped to fuel my car today at a BP station on Highway 67 at the Kentucky Avenue exit off I-465 and found myself back in Calvertville. Memories of long ago tapped on my window, I touched the unlock button and they came inside to sit a spell. Reminiscence is a vehicle that travels through time at the speed of light and doesn't cost anything for the ticket. I was engulfed with a cloud of memories that warmed my heart and took me back to a time and place that I didn't want to leave for a while. Three aspects of the experience placed me in the Model A Ford for the trip down memory lane: pumping my own gas, the railroad bridge and a Coca Cola.

When I was in my salad days, my entire life revolved around the farm and Calvertville, Indiana. Calvertville was a country store, a feed mill, the Concord Baptist Church, a two-room school [it was brick not log cabin] and a sawmill. The Martindale family operated the store and the mill. The concrete block store building had a large porch on the front next to the road with two Standard Oil gas pumps. The pumps had glass cylinders on the top with gallon markings and glass crowns on the top of the cylinder. Customers purchased gasoline by the gallon not by the amount of money. Gasoline cost 20 cents per gallon.

Ralph would grasp a handle on the side of the pump much like a slot machine handle and pump the gas into the glass cylinder and then let gravity feed it into your gas tank. If you would have told me then that in the future people would pump their own gas and pay for it using a plastic card at the pump I would have laughed and said that you were a quart or so less than a gallon. I thought about Ralph and the store as I pumped my own gas and used my debit card. The gas cost $2.50 per gallon.

There is a steel railroad bridge that spans High School Road a stones throw from that station. The street makes a turn to go under it and continues north where it is all but lost in the maze that has become Indianapolis International Airport and the influence of I-465. As I looked at the bridge I remembered Harold McIntosh, his school bus and the state fair.

Mac was the school bus driver all the years I went to school. The first day my brother and I walked to the mailbox and waited for the bus, he swooped down the road in his big yellow juggernaut, flipped open the door and with a grin bigger than outside said, "Howdy, get on here and let's go to school." Twelve years later he was still driving and for many years after that. If you were to travel from Spencer to Pottersville Farm, New Hope and Vilas and on to Jack's Creek Bridge then turn right on the Farmer's Ferry road, he lived down there a ways.

Each year Mac would take paying customers to the state fair. We would leave the Calvertville store before daylight and pick up more people in Worthington. We then traveled north on highway 67 to High School Road and passed under that same bridge, went north to 38th street and east to the fairgrounds. My eyes got so big I could have been in a Disney Movie when I saw the lights, sights and sounds of the fair.

In days of yore I would go into the Calvertville Store and purchase a six-ounce bottle of Coca Cola and a bag of Planters Peanuts for ten cents, one thin dime. The red Coke box had a hinged lid that would open on either end. I would extract a "kokoller" from the cold water, pop the cap off in the opener on the front of the box, pour the peanuts into the bottle and go to Nirvana for a little while. I didn't know where Nirvana was but it tasted good.

That day I went inside and purchased a 20-ounce coke for $1.19. It was in a refrigerated cooler, in a plastic bottle, diet and caffeine free. It was delicious; just as I remembered. However, it has been so long since I drank a regular coke I don't remember how it is supposed to taste. It is the same with cheese, bacon, whole milk and butter.

I did some math. If a coke cost me a nickel for six ounces back then that is less than a penny an ounce. Reason would dictate that today a 20-ounce coke should cost me about nineteen cents. If not, why not? I believe that I was overcharged by a dollar.

As a kid I had no money of my own. I was never paid an allowance nor was I paid for working on the farm. I only had money when my parents gave it to me. The $1.19 made no impact on my economic status but back then I scarcely ever had two dimes to rub together.

After a few minutes of reverie I had to move because a well meaning man behind me began blowing his horn and loudly yelping hurtful things about my ancestry.

Noah and His Ark 2005

You think the first Noah had trouble? Fast forward to Noah - 2005. Noah is presenting his plans to build an ark, a large ship, 450 feet long, 75 feet wide and 45 feet high with three decks, to carry people and animals to escape an impending flood.

The county planning officer asked, "May I see your plans for the ship?" "Plans?" "I only build as the Lord instructs me." "The Lord?" "Is he on the planning commission?" "Mr. Noah, there must be sufficient heating, ventilation and air conditioning to maintain proper temperatures. The ventilation system must provide each person and each large animal a minimum of 1600 cubic feet of fresh air every 24 hours. Each person must also have a minimum of 150 square feet of living space and each animal, at least 50 square feet of space. Will your vessel provide such?"

Officials from the Indiana Department of Environmental Matters and Environmental Protection Agency took the podium. "Mr. Noah, how do you plan to treat the sewage and waste products that these animals and humans will produce each day? May we see your plan that shows the proper treatment of effluent so its disposal will not adversely impact the environment?" "We had just planned to toss it overboard as needed. There will be sufficient water to dilute it." "That is an unacceptable plan. You must file a plan with our offices within 60 days or we will shut you down."

The state health authority delegate then spoke. "Mr. Noah, how many foot candles of natural light will be available on your ship? How many foot candles of artificial light will be provided for each human and each animal?" "There will be an opening 18 inches high along the top of ship but I don't know how much light that will let in. We planned on using candles when needed." Mr. Noah, each human must be provided with a minimum of 10 foot candles of light and each animal five." "Oh."

The fire marshal then asked, "What mode of ingress and egress is available in case there is a need to evacuate in an emergency?" "There will only be one door and it will be closed and tightly secured against water leakage." "Mr. Noah, in a vessel this size, there must be a minimum of 10 emergency exits on each side of the vessel, clearly marked with lighted red exit signs and equipped with crash bars for easy egress. What plans do you have for a sprinkler system in the event of fire? "I thought an egress was a bird."

The county health officer then spoke, "Mr. Noah, what provisions have you made for storing dry food and refrigeration for perishables and potable water?" "We had not planned for such situations because we planned on taking dried foods and grains." "And just how were you planning to prepare the food? We must have a plan before the project moves forward."

The local chapter of PETA then asked, "What plans do you have for housing the animals in appropriate spaces with sufficient food and space to exercise and medical treatment?" "We just thought we would place them in holding pens." "Current law requires proper ventilation, an exercise area, a properly licensed veterinarian for each 100 animals and proper inoculations because of the proximity of the animals to each other. Further, each animal must have a one-year supply of forage, grain and ample supply of fresh potable water."

The ADA representative then asked, "What plans have you made to address the needs of those humans and animals who have handicaps or disabilities and cannot function without accommodations?" "I hadn't thought about that." "We require a plan to address such needs as ramps, drinking facilities and restrooms before this project can go forward."

The local bar association then queried, "Mr. Noah, do you have an approved policy of indemnification for you and your family against any foreseeable law suits, injuries suffered by negligence and Acts of God" "No. Is that required?" "We highly recommend it or you will be culpable for many possible accidents. Do you have an errors and omissions policy in your adopted operations manual?"

The state superintendent of public education then asked, "What plans do you have in place for educating the children of school age while on this voyage? You are required to provide an education for children any time they are not enrolled in school."

The county planning commission then stated, "the area you are planning to build this vessel is not zoned for shipbuilding. People are also worried that this will have a negative impact on their property values. It is zoned for agriculture and light industry so you must cease and desist from building on the proposed site."

The trade unions then spoke. "Do you plan to use union labor on the construction of this vessel and the equipping and outfitting of the interior? The union steward will visit the site to make that determination and inspect the working conditions."

Noah said, "Lord, what is plan B?"

The New Alphabet

[This poem came in through the transom. It was written by Anon, the most prolific writer in the history of the world.]

A is for apple, and B is for boat
That used to be right, but now it won't float!
Age before beauty is what we once said,
But let's be a bit more realistic instead.

A is for arthritis,
B is the bad back,
C is the chest pains, perhaps cardiac?
D is for dentures, decay and decline,
E is for eyesight, I can't read that top line!

F is for fissures and fluid retention,
G is for gas which I'd rather not mention,
H is high blood pressure – I'd rather it be low,

I is for incisions with scars you can show,
J is for joints, out of socket, won't mend,
K is for knees that crack when they bend,
L is for libido, where did it go?
M is for memory, I don't remember you know.

N is neuralgia, in nerves way down low,
O is for osteo, the bones that don't grow!
P is for prescriptions, I have quite a few,
just give me a pill and I'll be as good as new.

Q is for queasy, is it fatal or flu?
R is for reflux, one meal turns to two.
S is for sleepless nights, counting my fears,
T is for Tinnitus, for the bells in my ears!

U is for urinary, big troubles with flow,
V is for vertigo, that's dizzy you know,
W is for worry, now what's going 'round?
X is for X-ray and what might be found.

Y is another year that is left behind,
Z is for zest that I still have in my mind.
I've survived all the symptoms my body's
deployed, and I've kept twenty-six doctors fully
employed!
[**Note:** I bought a new Cadillac this year. The
only problem is that my doctor is driving it instead
of me.]

Together on the Hill Again

In 1940, the year before America officially entered W.W. II, my parents purchased several plots in the Calvertville Cemetery. It is my understanding they purchased them from my grandma Van. The cemetery, a small, quiet halcyon location, is located on a hill west of downtown Calvertville. For as long as my memory serves, there has been a sandstone archway at the entrance. A walk about causes a stroll down memory lane. It is a history book of my past. People that I knew years ago lie together in quiet repose.

On that day in 1940 my parents didn't need plots for themselves and wouldn't for many years. They knew intellectually that some day they would but psychologically that day seemed 10,000 years away. However, they did need a place to bury an infant son, Richard. Dad was 32 and Mom was 24. I will never know the grief they experienced that day. I was about two and unaware of what was happening. Thankfully both of our daughters lived to adulthood and are still living. I have traveled the road to the cemetery with others who have lost infants and children and it is the most sorrowful experience that humans must endure.

Death runs in my family; a stalker. The sun rises and sets, day follows day, month follows month and year follows year and before you know it you step into old age and the day arrives. Such was the day eight years ago when The Grim Reaper came for my dad. The weight of 89 years and a life of commitment and duty weighed heavily upon his shoulders. Death promised a way of escaping those worldly burdens and together they walked the long corridor and dad joined his son on the hill. I'm sure those 57 intervening years since the time the plots were purchased passed rapidly. Looking forward 57 years seems like an eternity. Looking backward, 57 years seems like a short time. I can testify to that.

For the next six years Mom lived contentedly on the farm they purchased in 1941. But during that sixth year the Grim Reaper began stalking her. We had to place her in a nursing home. For the first few months she knew where she was but she didn't understand why she was there. The day we admitted her my sister and brother were taking care of the paperwork and business matters and I was standing in the hallway with Mom. We were talking about everything and nothing and in a sudden moment of clarity she began to realize that she was going to be living there, and she said, "I must have been a mean old mother." I could barely see or talk at that moment. I put my arm around her frail shoulders and tried my best to bolster her up and convince her that she was the best mother in the world. I tried to reassure her that this was the best place for her to be. I tried in vain to dispel her fears and make her feel loved and needed. I am not sure she was convinced. That made me very sad.

After a struggle she adjusted to her situation. One day she said, "I know I'm not at home, but I'm not sure where I am." She became so thin and frail that she didn't look like my mother any more. We talked but I couldn't understand what she was saying. Sometimes I believe that she understood what I said but I'm not sure. Perhaps it is because that is what I wanted to believe. She maintained her sense of humor to the end. When I visited she always smiled at me and I hope that meant she recognized who I was.

For the 18 months she was in the nursing home The Grim Reaper hung around the yard. He pecked on the window many times. A few times he reached for the doorknob only to pull back and delay his entrance. In February of 2005 he brashly strode through the door grasped her hand and Mom laid down the burdens of this life, cast off the shell of her earthly body and together they walked the same corridor that he and Dad used and she joined her beloved husband and son on the hill. Try as we might we could not prevent the journey and we could not bring her back.

I was grieved and relieved simultaneously. It was painful for me, release for her. That sounds calloused and it might be. But over the past year and a half she did not enjoy much quality in her life. Although she did not suffer and she was not in pain, the weight of 89 years and her illness wore her out physically and emotionally. She had to be cared for in every aspect of her life. That was a crushing blow to one who gave her life to caring for her family and then taking care of herself as long as she could. The only consoling aspect is that she was not aware of what was happening to her. Nancy Reagan was right. Alzheimer's is a crippling disease that took Mom to a place where we could no longer reach her. Thank you Mom for being a wonderful mother, grandmother and great grandmother.

Grandpa Knows Where Things Usta Be

I was talking to an eleven-year-old boy recently and he said, "I like to ride with my Grandpa in his old pickup truck, Faith. He calls the truck that because he says it has hauled a mountain of stuff. His old truck smells like a farm. He carries stuff in it like chains, a hammer, jack, chainsaw, a half sack of fertilizer, a shovel, some boards, a roll of barbed wire and three bricks. There are always a lot of papers on the dashboard. He knows where things usta be and where important places are now." That conversation made me think about my Grandpa Price and Grandpas in general.

- Grandpa knows where things usta be: "That usta be a barber shop and that building over there usta be the Farmall Implement Dealer. This usta be Clark's farm before it was a shopping center."
- Grandpa knows where all of the ice cream stores are and he always has money to buy me an ice cream cone.
- Grandpa can fix almost anything and he uses old tools that he got from his dad or his grandpa.
- Grandpa always walks slowly so I can keep up without running. He also likes to sit down and rest when I get tired.
- Grandpa always has a fishing pole ready and he knows where to fish. We don't always catch fish but we have fun trying.
- Grandpa knows what a squirrel sounds like when it barks and chatters way up in the trees. He also knows the difference between rabbit, squirrel and raccoon tracks in the snow.
- Grandpa always lets me saw the board with his old handsaw even though I don't always get it straight. He helps me push the saw through the board and no matter how it turns out; it is always a good job.

- Grandpa always lets me look for things in his shop because he says my eyes are better than his.
- Grandpa doesn't have a job so he can mow the yard anytime he wants to.
- Grandpa knows how to grow the best garden that is filled with tomatoes, green beans, cabbage, lettuce and potatoes.
- Grandpa showed me how to drive a nail with his old wooden handled hammer. He said if I had a dollar for every nail that hammer had driven I would not have to worry about college tuition.
- Grandpa has a heavy winter coat that he lets me wear because he is afraid I will get cold.
- Grandpa lets me wear his gum boots when it rains because he thinks my feet might get wet.
- Grandpa gave me a John Deere cap to wear when the sun is really hot because he says, "Men wear caps."
- Grandpa wears a thick sweater when it gets cool and I like to snuggle up next to him to keep warm.
- Grandpa wears old wire rimmed glasses so he can see to do his chores. They are scratched and bent but he says he likes them that way.

- Grandpa can name every president since Abraham Lincoln but he can't remember all the names of his grandchildren.
- Grandpa is a good listener. He looks at me and listens to my stories and he answers every question that I can think of about stuff.
- Grandpa is an older dad. They walk alike, talk alike and look alike.
- Grandpa thinks that he and I should take a nap every day and sometimes he is asleep before I am.
- Grandpa wears old shoes and socks because he says they are comfortable and they are broken in real good.
- Grandpa knows where the good mushrooms grow even though they don't sometimes.
- Grandpa doesn't know the correct address of very many places but he never gets lost and he can take you everywhere you need to go.
- Grandpa makes the best homemade ice cream in the world and he lets me turn the crank until I get tired; grandma helps some in the kitchen.
- Grandpa and I were building a frame the other day and I accidentally broke the glass in his level. He said, "That's all right son, when men work they break things sometimes."

- Grandpa doesn't run much. He says that he has hurried enough in his life and he thinks it is time to sit and watch other people hurry.
- Grandpa doesn't know how to work a computer. He says the best computer is a Graphite Ticonderoga 200. That's what he calls his pencil.
- Grandpa said he doesn't need a cell phone because he never has been and doesn't plan to ever be in jail.

A Few Of My Favorite Things

[Sung to the tune of My Favorite Things from Sound of Music]

Maalox and nose drops and needles for knitting,
Walkers and handrails and a new dental fitting,
Bundles of magazines tied up with string,
These are a few of my favorite things.

Cadillacs and cataracts and hearing aids and glasses,
Polident and Fixodent and false teeth in glasses,
Pacemaker, golf carts and porches with swings,
These are a few of my favorite things.

When the pipes leak,
When the bones creak,
When the knees go bad,
Then I remember my favorite things,
And then I don't feel so bad.

Hot tea and crumpets and corn pads for bunions,
No spicy hot food and no food with onions,
Bathrobes and heat pads and hot meals they bring,
These are a few of my favorite things.

Back pains, confused brains and no fear of sinnin',
Thin bones and fractures and hair that is thinnin',
And we won't mention our short shrunken frames
When we remember our favorite things.

When the joints ache,
When the hips break,
When the eyes grow dim,
Then I remember the great life I've had,
And then I don't feel so bad.

Claude Pepper, We Are Here

[If you do not know who Claude Pepper was, stop reading now because the rest of the article will not amuse you. I mean it. Stop reading now. If you continue reading, the staff and management of this book or its publisher will not assume any liability for the consequences you may suffer and we will disavow any right to litigation on your behalf. See the disclaimer at the front of the book and note the name of the law firm that represents me.]

I received my first **AARP** (American Association of Retired Persons) card when I reached the age of 50. It really was my rude introduction to Geezerdom. It didn't matter that I had not and did not plan to retire then. I am not proud, though, I gladly accepted the benefits the magic card provided. Membership provides discounts on motel rooms and some airline tickets, discounts in some restaurants and theaters, lower car insurance, prescription drug delivery to your door at a lower price and information on how to purchase a scooter or to determine if you qualify to have it paid for by Medicare. Now I just ask clerks and other service personnel to use my face as verification that I am a senior citizen - Geezer. No one has challenged me in many years.

In recent years BW and I have concluded that Geezers like to travel in the "off season". We made that conclusion last October when we were in Branson, Missouri, the Mecca of ambulatory Geezers of America. Why do you think we were there? Geezers can travel then because they are retired and have earned the right to take a trip anywhere they please anytime they please. There should be some benefit to living a long time, don't you agree?

Geezers were everywhere. There is more gray hair in Branson in October than there is snow on the Matterhorn in January. Branson streets and venues resemble a white out in a blizzard from September through December. Those life time membership AARP cards were getting heat rash and razor burn from being whipped through the scanners at the malls and restaurants and being presented for discounts at motels and RV parks. Some disappeared in a cloud of smoke because of spontaneous combustion. Most stores have a barrel of water near the cash register to serve as a coolant. It reminded me of Gar Wells' blacksmith shop in my hometown of Worthington, Indiana, years ago. Steam would fly and the water would hiss when he put horseshoes and plowshares in the water barrel to cool them.

Geezers are the reason that the has-beens of the entertainment world are fixtures in Branson. Geezers are the only ones who know or remember Bobby Vinton, Andy Williams, Jim Stafford, The Osmond Brothers, Tony Orlando and Dawn, The Lawrence Welk Show, Mickey Gilley and Mel Tillis. They all have their AARP cards too and most of them have restrictions on their driver's license that prohibits them from driving after dark. That is why their shows end so early.

There were so many fifth wheel campers, RVs, tent campers and other styles of camper vehicles in town that it looked like a RV dealership on the move. On the road to Branson we passed so many that it looked like the Union Pacific Railroad Line.

Larry Vandeventer

We never saw so many double knit suits, double knit pants, horn rim glasses, hard side suitcases and overnight cases since the 1970's or was it in Florida the winter before?

I'll bet my next paycheck against yours that there were more pacemakers than pace arrows in town. There was enough nitroglycerine and cholesterol lowering medicine in pockets and purses to stock a regional distribution center for CVS Drug Stores. Sales of Kaopectate and Milk of Magnesia are the highest per capita there than anywhere except Florida and Sun City, Arizona. Senior citizen drug pushers blatantly sell over-the-counter drugs out of the trunks of their cars right there on the streets. Every restaurant and buffet line has drums of industrial strength Pepto-Bismol at the cash register.

Traffic is terribly congested in Branson. It is slower than a tax refund. It takes longer to drive a block in Branson than it took for the 2000 presidential election. There is a local law that states: "No driver shall exceed five miles per hour; drivers must hold one foot on the brake pedal with the brake lights on just in case they may stop in the next 30 minutes; drivers must keep at least one turn signal blinking just in case they might want to turn sometime in the next three hours. If a driver is unsure of which way he or she is going to turn, then said driver must keep the hazard lights flashing just in case. Stopping in the middle of the road to read maps and determine the location of the next buffet is permissible as long as you intend to move on in the next two hours."

We noticed that there is no late nightlife in Branson. Everything closes after Andy Williams' last show. Silver Dollar City closes at 5:00 to insure that all ticket holders can get back to town in time to take their Prilosec and Lipitor tablets before dinner. The streetlights go off at 9:00 p.m. Senior citizens on the streets after that are given a free ride in the nice policeman's car or the local 911-rescue unit to the nearest medical facility because it is assumed that they must be confused and lost.

BW and I will go to Branson again this fall but I must get my leisure suits washed and ironed before we go. I also have to get my prescription of Lipitor renewed. It seems that one of our turn signal bulbs is burned out too.

(The late **Claude Pepper was a congressional leader from Florida who was a champion for senior citizens and their rights. I knew you wouldn't stop reading.)**

About The Author

Dr. Larry Vandeventer was born at home in Ghost Hollow, Indiana, 13.2 lustrums ago. His education began in a two-room country school in Calvertville, Indiana and he eventually attained a Ph.D. from Indiana State University.

He and Wanda have been married more than nine lustrums and they have two married, professional daughters: TW who is married to Keith and TM who is married to Todd and they have one child, a perfect and well-advanced four-year old granddaughter. Another is expected. Hooray! It is our hope that this one knows about calendars and time.

His work life has been varied working as a farm hand, as a service station attendant, as a custodian while in college, in banking, served in U.S. Navy and as a full-time minister.

He has also been a public school teacher, high school assistant principal and later a principal and assistant superintendent. Currently he is a professor of graduate and post-graduate education, newspaper columnist and author. Who said nothing good could come out of hills of Highland Township? The jury is still out on that one.

At this stage in his life he does pretty much what he wants to and doesn't get started on that until he feels like it.

To Order Copies of These Books

There are three ways to order copies of Larry Vandeventer's books: (1) Contact *Author House Publishing at AuthorHouse.com or 1663 Liberty Drive, Suite 200, Bloomington, IN 47403, 1-888-519-5121, (2) Order through your local bookstore, (3) Contact me to get an autographed copy by completing the form below and mailing it to:

Larry Vandeventer
6860 Sunrise Drive
Plainfield, IN 46168
Phone 317-839-7656
E-mail Goosecrick@aol.com

Please send me:

_____Copies of <u>You Might Be A Geezer</u> @ $12.95 each.

_____Copies of <u>There is a Booger in There and Other Little Audrey Stories</u> @ $12.95 each.

_____Copies of <u>Bumps In The Road [Things I Have Run Across]</u> @ $19.95 each.

_____Copies of <u>Life In The Past Lane</u> @ $14.95 each.

[**Note**: Add 6% Sales Tax, plus $3.50 S & H for each book.]

_____Copies of the books on 3.5 inch floppy diskette

_____Copies of the CD with Five books on it.

[***Note***: All three books are available on 3.5 inch floppy diskettes for $5.00 each plus $2.00 shipping and handling each. Microsoft WordXP format]

All four books plus two other unpublished books are available on a CD also in Microsoft Word XP. The CD sells for $20.00 plus $3.50 shipping and handling.

_____

Your Name

_____

Address   City

_____

City   State Zip   Telephone

SEND A GIFT COPY TO A FRIEND
Autograph to
Name and Address of the friend [Print Please]

www.ingramcontent.com/pod-product-compliance
Lightning Source LLC
Chambersburg PA
CBHW061348280526
45784CB00001B/181